FUND DIRECTOR'S GUIDEBOOK

4TH EDITION

D1602434

Federal Regulation of Securities Committee

Business Law Section

Printed in the United States of America.

19   18   17   16   15   5   4   3   2   1

Library of Congress Cataloging-in-Publication Data

Fund director's guidebook — Fourth edition.
    pages cm
  Includes index.
  ISBN 978-1-63425-265-2 (alk. paper)
  1. Mutual funds—Law and legislation—United States.   2. Closed-end funds—Law and legislation—United States.   3. Directors of corporations—Legal status, laws, etc.—United States.   I. Title.

  KF1078.S36 2016
  346.73′06642—dc23

                                                                    2015030703

Contents

Foreword

This is the fourth edition of the American Bar Association Section of Business Law's *Fund Director's Guidebook* (the "Guidebook"). It is intended to assist directors of investment companies registered under the Investment Company Act of 1940 (the "1940 Act") in fulfilling their responsibilities. The Guidebook should be useful to directors of both open-end investment companies (typically referred to as mutual funds) and closed-end funds. The Guidebook was inspired in part by the *Corporate Director's Guidebook*, which was originally published by the Section of Business Law in 1978 and most recently updated with the sixth edition in 2011.

The Guidebook was initially published in 1996 and updated in 2003 with the publication of the second edition and in 2006 with the publication of the third edition. The second edition reflected a number of significant developments that had occurred since 1996 affecting the responsibilities of fund directors, particularly the enactment of the Sarbanes-Oxley Act of 2002 (the "Sarbanes-Oxley Act"). The third edition primarily reflected a broad range of reform initiatives undertaken by the Securities and Exchange Commission (the "SEC") in response to mutual fund trading abuses occurring in 2003 and 2004. These reforms resulted in significant changes in the manner in which funds, fund directors, and their service providers conduct business. The SEC reform package included expanded governance provisions designed to enhance the independence and effectiveness of fund boards; a new compliance rule mandating a comprehensive compliance regimen for funds, advisers, and certain other service providers; and expanded disclosure requirements in a number of areas.

Since 2006, there have been significant developments affecting funds in the wake of the 2008–2009 financial crisis and the resulting legislation, the Dodd-Frank Wall Street Reform and Consumer Protection Act of 2010 (the "Dodd-Frank Act"). Among other things, there has been increased civil litigation involving funds and their service providers, and a more active role of the SEC and its staff in asserting securities law fund-related violations, including SEC enforcement actions against independent directors brought under the 1940 Act's compliance rule. There also has been an emphasis by the SEC on what has been described as a "gatekeeper" role that independent directors play, an increased focus on the activities of money market funds (including two major rulemakings by the SEC), and a renewed focus by the SEC on the use of third-party intermediaries to distribute and service funds and the compensation received by the intermediaries for these services. The industry has also experienced tremendous growth in exchange-traded funds and funds that use alternative investment strategies.

This Guidebook uses the terms "fund" and "investment company" interchangeably. These terms also encompass each portfolio in the case of a series fund. In addition, for convenience, the Guidebook uses the terms "director" and "board of directors" even though many funds are organized as business trusts and thus have "trustees" and a "board of trustees." The term "independent directors" means directors who are not "interested persons" of the fund as defined in Section 2(a)(19) of the 1940 Act, and the term "inside directors" means directors who are "interested persons." Statements made about directors and their responsibilities under the 1940 Act apply equally to trustees. In addition, the terms "investment advisory contract" and "investment management agreement" refer to the contractual arrangements between the fund and its investment adviser or manager that govern the provision of investment advisory and management services. The Guidebook covers open-end funds, closed-end funds and exchange-traded funds. Closed-end funds differ from open-end funds in that they do not stand ready to redeem their shares daily at net asset value and generally do not engage in continuous public offerings of their shares. Shares of closed-end funds are traded in the market and may be listed on stock exchanges. Exchange-traded funds (or ETFs) often are structured as open-end funds, but trade their shares on securities exchanges in a manner similar to shares of listed closed-end funds. The differences between open-end, closed-end, and exchange-traded funds are discussed in Sections 13 and 14. For convenience, commonly used investment company terms are defined in the Glossary.

Task Force on *Fund Director's Guidebook*, Federal Regulation of Securities Committee, Fourth Edition

Co-Chairs: Andrew J. Donohue, New York, NY
Lori L. Schneider, Washington, DC
Thomas R. Smith, Jr., New York, NY

Jay G. Baris, New York, NY
Rajib Chanda, Washington, D.C.
Sarah E. Cogan, New York, NY
Donald R. Crawshaw, New York, NY
Alison M. Fuller, Washington, D.C.
Nathan J. Greene, New York, NY
James J. Hanks, Jr., Baltimore, MD
Arthur B. Laby, Camden, NJ
Timothy W. Levin, Philadelphia, PA
John A. MacKinnon, New York, NY
Janna Manes, New York, NY
Lori A. Martin, New York, NY
Margery K. Neale, New York, NY
John F. Olson, Washington, D.C.
Paulita A. Pike, Chicago, IL
Robert A. Robertson, Newport Beach, CA
Eric D. Roiter, Boston, MA
David A. Sturms, Chicago, IL
Craig S. Tyle, San Mateo, CA

SECTION **1**

Background and Structure of the Guidebook

The 1940 Act is a pervasive regulatory regime that contemplates an important and active role for fund directors. Consequently, fund directors should have a basic understanding of relevant 1940 Act provisions and of the scope and nature of their duties and responsibilities. Although fund managers and shareholders have common interests in many areas, there are potential conflicts of interest between the two. Under the 1940 Act regulatory framework, the fund directors (particularly the independent directors) are responsible for monitoring potential conflicts and representing the interests of shareholders. Although they generally work closely and cooperatively with fund management, the independent directors must exercise independent judgment.

The role of the board of directors of funds differs in certain important respects from the role of the board of directors of an operating company; this is because of the external management structure typical of most investment companies. A fund is usually organized by a "sponsor," such as an investment management company, securities firm, or financial institution. Investment advisory, administrative, distribution, and other operational services are provided to the fund through contractual arrangements with service providers, some or all of which are typically affiliates of the sponsor. In addition, the fund's officers are usually provided, employed, and compensated by the fund's investment adviser or administrator. The adviser necessarily operates its business in its own best interests, which may not always be congruent with the best interests of the fund's shareholders. It is the independent directors' responsibility to represent the interests of fund shareholders where those interests might be in conflict with those of the adviser.

This Guidebook provides an overview of the functions, responsibilities, and potential liabilities of fund directors, both under the federal securities laws (including the 1940 Act) and corporate law. It also provides information about the structure and operations of the board and its relationship to the investment adviser, the distributor, and others important to the fund. This book is intended to assist directors in discharging their responsibilities by providing them with enough information to understand their duties and to ask the right questions. It is not intended to provide all the answers. Perhaps even more than the typical corporate director, fund directors should regularly seek and rely upon the advice of legal counsel due to the comprehensive regulation funds are subject to and the externalization of management at most funds.

This Guidebook offers suggestions as to how independent directors can best fulfill their responsibilities by referencing industry practice, legal requirements, and the experiences and perspectives of the members of the Task Force who drafted the Guidebook. It must be emphasized, however, that there is no single way that independent directors can best fulfill their responsibilities, and there is often no one preferred approach to many of the matters discussed in the Guidebook. Furthermore, the positions taken in the Guidebook do not necessarily reflect the views of every Task Force member in all matters. The suggestions and positions discussed in the Guidebook are believed to be current as of July 31, 2015.

Regulatory Overview

A. The Legal Framework

Investment companies are registered with the SEC under the 1940 Act, which contains stringent and comprehensive provisions that require strict adherence to stated investment policies and limitations, prohibits certain types of investments, restricts transactions with affiliates, and regulates investment advisory and distribution arrangements. Regulation extends to such matters as composition of the board and election of directors, capital structure, portfolio transactions, custodial arrangements, fidelity bonding, selection of accountants, compliance programs, valuation and pricing of shares, and portfolio liquidity. The 1940 Act also contains extensive record-keeping requirements and contemplates that the SEC will regularly conduct inspections of investment advisers, distributors, and funds.

The SEC has broad enforcement authority and a wide range of enforcement remedies through which it may impose significant penalties upon fund service providers, fund officers, and fund directors. The SEC is, however, a civil law enforcement agency, and it does not have the authority to bring criminal actions.

The SEC regulates investment advisers to investment companies under the Investment Advisers Act of 1940 (the "Advisers Act"). As in the case of the 1940 Act, all references to the various Acts under the federal securities laws discussed herein are deemed to include the rules and regulations thereunder. The Advisers Act contains a few basic requirements, such as registration with the SEC, maintenance of certain business records, and delivery to clients of a disclosure statement. Most significant is a provision of the Advisers Act that prohibits advisers from defrauding their clients, a provision that has been construed as imposing on advisers a general fiduciary obligation to their clients. This fiduciary duty requires advisers to manage their clients' portfolios in the best interests of clients. A number of obligations to clients flow from this fiduciary duty, including the duty to fully disclose any material conflicts the adviser has with its clients, to seek best execution for client transactions, and to have a reasonable basis for client recommendations. Fund activities are also subject to other federal laws, notably the Securities Act of 1933 (the "1933 Act") and the Securities Exchange Act of 1934 (the "1934 Act"). Depending on whether or not a fund trades commodity interests, its activities, and those of its investment adviser, may be subject to the jurisdiction of the Commodity Futures Trading Commission ("CFTC") and the Commodity Exchange Act (the "CEA"). The CEA and the role of the CFTC with respect to funds are discussed in Section 2.D below.

Funds that are publicly available are registered with the SEC under both the 1933 Act and the 1940 Act. The 1933 Act is primarily a disclosure statute designed to ensure that investors are provided with full and fair disclosure of material information concerning securities offerings and issuers, including funds. Funds must register offerings of their securities with the SEC by filing a registration statement that includes the fund's prospectus and Statement of Additional Information ("SAI"). The 1934 Act regulates the securities markets and broker-dealers, imposes reporting and proxy requirements on public companies (including funds), and prohibits fraud or manipulation in the purchase or sale of securities. The Financial Industry Regulatory Authority ("FINRA"), a self-regulatory organization, regulates, among other things, the sales practices of broker-dealers selling shares of funds. The offer and sale of fund shares may also be subject to notice filing requirements and anti-fraud prohibitions under state laws.

Despite heightened focus upon the responsibilities of independent directors, the role of directors is to provide oversight, and not management. Unless provided otherwise, fund management should be an active participant in the decision-making process, even when the board or the audit committee has the duty to make the decision or determination. In this regard, it is entirely appropriate for management to make recommendations based upon its knowledge and experience gained through the day-to-day management of the fund.

Investment companies are typically organized as corporations or trusts under the laws of a particular state. Directors of investment companies are subject to traditional standards of director responsibility under state statutes and common law. Although funds are organized under the laws of a number of states, many funds organized in corporate form are organized under the laws of Maryland, and many funds organized as trusts are organized as Massachusetts business trusts or Delaware statutory trusts. The responsibilities and duties of fund directors under state law are discussed in Section 3.A.

The regulatory regime makes possible many and varied sources of liability for fund directors and officers and service providers, particularly the investment adviser and the distributor (or principal underwriter) of the fund's shares. Liabilities may arise from private litigation or SEC, state or other regulatory proceedings. Historically, management, including the inside directors, has been more likely than the independent directors to be the target of private litigation or regulatory proceedings. However, in 2010 the SEC greatly strengthened its enforcement program with the creation of an asset management unit. Since 2013, there have been a few different SEC enforcement proceedings in which fund directors (including independent directors) were sanctioned. These initiatives by the SEC make important greater scrutiny of directors' indemnification and insurance. (see Section 16).

B. Structure of the Typical Fund and Role of the Independent Director

Most U.S. investment companies are externally managed, and typically all service arrangements necessary for the operation of the fund are provided by separate legal entities. The fund sponsor (or an affiliate thereof) normally becomes the fund's investment adviser and the distributor. Other models also exist. Some fund sponsors act as "managers of managers" and, while serving as investment adviser or manager to their funds, outsource all or some of the investment advisory services to sub-advisers. In addition, some fund service providers offer a "platform" to unaffiliated investment advisers who wish to enter the fund business without incurring the substantial costs of establishing the compliance, distribution, shareholder servicing, and other infrastructure of a fund complex. It is the statutory responsibility of the directors of the fund—particularly the independent directors—to regularly review and approve the arrangements with entities selected to provide portfolio management, distribution services, and various other services required to operate the fund. The directors are responsible for monitoring the potential conflicts of interest between fund management and fund shareholders and for representing the interests of the shareholders. Directors—particularly the independent directors—also have significant oversight and monitoring responsibilities under both state law and the federal securities laws (see Sections 3 and 7).

Under the 1940 Act, the independent directors of a fund play a vital role. The Supreme Court of the United States summarized that role in *Burks v. Lasker,* 441 U.S. 471, 484–85 (1979) (citations omitted):

> Congress' purpose in structuring the 1940 Act as it did is clear. It was designed to place the unaffiliated directors in the role of 'independent watchdogs,' who would furnish an independent check upon the management of investment companies.

In short, the structure and purpose of the 1940 Act indicate that Congress entrusted to the independent directors of investment companies, exercising the authority granted to them by state law, the primary responsibility for looking after the interests of the fund's shareholders.

C. Increased Regulatory Scrutiny by the SEC and Increase in Civil Litigation

The SEC expects the independent directors to monitor the funds' activities and protect the interests of shareholders. The manner in which the independent directors perform their duties is of paramount importance to the SEC. In response to mutual fund trading abuses in 2003 and 2004, the SEC adopted a series of reforms containing, among other things, significant fund governance reforms (including a mandatory chief compliance officer position for funds and a written compliance policies and procedures requirement for funds, advisers and certain other service providers) and expanded disclosure provisions in a number of areas (including expanded disclosure of the material factors and conclusions that form the basis for approval by fund boards of investment advisory agreements). These reforms were designed to enhance substantially the independence and effectiveness of fund boards.

Over the past number of years, independent fund directors have become subject to an increased level of scrutiny from fund shareholders, regulators, and fund industry observers, including the media. Industry critics claim that fund directors too rarely oppose management, while some industry observers question whether the SEC's reform initiatives place excessive burdens of time and responsibility on the independent directors and risk involving the directors in management activities rather than oversight.

This increased regulatory scrutiny has continued following the 2008–2009 financial crisis, with increasing focus on money market fund reform, liquidity, valuation, compliance programs, risk management programs, the use of derivatives and alternative strategies, the systemic risks of particular types of funds and the asset management industry as a whole, the structure of payments to intermediaries that sell or service funds, and an active SEC enforcement program.

In 2013, SEC Chair Mary Jo White expressed a new all-encompassing approach for the SEC's enforcement program, saying:

> One of our goals is to see that the SEC's enforcement program is—and is perceived to be—everywhere, pursuing all types of violations of our federal securities laws, big and small.

Chair White analogized her view to the "broken windows" approach to community policing—i.e., when a window is broken and someone fixes it, it is a sign that disorder will not be tolerated. But when a broken window "is not fixed it is a signal that no one cares, and so breaking more windows costs nothing."

Chair White further stated that the SEC is focusing more on those who play the role of "gatekeepers" in the financial system. She expressly discussed the role of investment company boards and recent SEC enforcement activity in this area, and indicated that board oversight of mutual funds will continue to be an area of enforcement emphasis, stating that:

> Investment company boards serve as critical gatekeepers and we will focus on ensuring that they appropriately perform their duties. . . . It has been suggested that our focus on gatekeepers may drive away those who would otherwise serve in these roles, for fear of being second-guessed or blamed for every issue that arises. . . . [But] being a director or in any similar role where you owe a fiduciary duty is not for the uninitiated or the faint of heart.

(See "Remarks by Chair Mary Jo White at the Securities Enforcement Forum," October 9, 2013.)

The SEC also has strengthened the manner in which it conducts surveillance of funds and advisers for compliance with the 1940 Act. In the SEC's inspection program, there is particular focus on assessing the quality of risk management procedures, internal controls, and compliance programs (see Section 9). In this regard, the SEC has established a "Compliance Program Initiative" pursuant to which the agency's enforcement staff have looked to bring actions based upon the failure to adopt or implement an adequate compliance program as required by Rule 38a-1 under the 1940 Act. Rule 38a-1 has become a mainstay for cases involving advisers and funds. Enforcement actions in this regard, unlike excessive fee cases, do not require the fund to have suffered any loss. The SEC staff is increasing its focus on the role of independent directors, looking for deficiencies on the part of directors in exercising their duties. As discussed in Section 5, in their enhanced examination program, the SEC staff is scrutinizing, among other things, the Section 15(c) process, in which boards approve advisory arrangements. Directors should remain aware of these initiatives and be kept apprised of future initiatives affecting funds and their directors, consulting legal counsel, and other appropriate advisors in the event that an SEC examination is undertaken or SEC staff contacts directors for questioning.

Civil litigation in the fund industry continues to be at a high level. There was a significant amount of litigation related to the market timing, late trading, and revenue sharing issues that first came to light in 2003. There was also a significant amount of litigation in the wake of the 2008–2009 financial crisis. Numerous class action lawsuits were brought alleging federal and state securities law violations, in addition to shareholder derivative actions asserting breach of fiduciary duty and mismanagement by fund advisers, officers, and directors. The fund industry has also been the target of FINRA arbitrations initiated by individual investors seeking to recoup losses incurred during the financial crisis. Settlements of these actions have resulted in hundreds of millions of dollars of costs to the investment management industry (primarily fund advisers) and its insurers, but not to funds themselves. While some of these cases remain, the plaintiffs' bar has moved onto new litigation targets. In particular, lawsuits alleging excessive fees under 1940 Act fiduciary standards have proliferated, although the Supreme Court has reined in these claims by confirming the heavy burden of proof required to demonstrate a breach of such standards. A number of lawsuits alleging that sub-advisory arrangements involve excessive fees to the fund's adviser (due to the difference between advisory and sub-advisory fees) have been filed in recent years, and several of them have survived motions to dismiss and advanced to discovery. Given the amounts involved in these and other cases, the fund industry is likely to remain a target of litigation for the foreseeable future.

Claims for relief against independent directors under the 1940 Act and state law are asserted from time to time, but have rarely succeeded to date. Although directors in general could be liable for claims of inadequate disclosures under the 1934 Act, independent directors often would not have the levels of control or scienter (i.e., knowledge of falsity or severe recklessness) required for those claims. Independent directors may be more vulnerable to certain claims under the 1933 Act, where they must affirmatively show that they acted with due diligence to avoid liability. However, courts addressing the due diligence defense have generally imposed lesser obligations on independent directors, while relying on a sliding scale approach that is based on the degree of a director's involvement in an offering, expertise, and access to pertinent information. Independent directors may also be subject to derivative claims brought on behalf of the fund by a shareholder alleging that the director's misconduct caused harm to the fund. The specific demand requirements for such claims are determined by the law of the fund's state of organization. Even when not named defendants, directors may be considered crucial witnesses in these cases. As scrutiny of the fund industry by the plaintiffs' bar continues, independent directors should carefully review and understand their legal responsibilities as directors as well as specific insurance coverage, including the nature and operation of any exclusions, retentions, limits of liability, notice of claim requirements, and arbitration provisions (if applicable), as well as the indemnification provisions of their funds' governing documents (see Section 16).

D. The CFTC

The CEA, and the CFTC's regulations thereunder, provide that pooled investment vehicles, such as funds, that trade "commodity interests" (defined to include commodity futures contracts and options thereon), as well as most swaps (but not including certain security-based swaps and certain foreign exchange contracts), are "commodity pools" unless an exclusion from the definition of commodity pool operator ("CPO") is available and claimed by the fund. The CFTC's position is that the investment adviser of a fund that is a commodity pool must be registered with the CFTC as a CPO. The fund's adviser must also be registered with the CFTC as a commodity trading adviser ("CTA") unless an exemption or exclusion is available. To the extent a fund has organized a wholly owned subsidiary to transact in commodity interests for federal income tax purposes, the operator of that entity (i.e., the adviser as a practical matter) is also considered to be a CPO by the CFTC, and the entity's adviser must be a CTA or exempt from registration as such. Note that the CFTC regulates the operator of a commodity pool (rather than regulating the commodity pool itself), whereas the SEC regulates the fund. However, the CFTC's rules directly impact a fund that is a commodity pool. (See Section 9 for a discussion of the compliance obligations of funds whose advisers must be registered CPOs.)

Funds that trade commodity interests below thresholds established in CFTC Rule 4.5 and comply with limitations on marketing and certain other requirements will not be subject to regulation as commodity pools—and their advisers will not be required to be registered CPOs—if they make a filing with the National Futures Association and update it on an annual basis. However, as a result of amendments to Rule 4.5 adopted by the CFTC in 2012, many funds that utilize commodity interests do not qualify for Rule 4.5 relief and are subject to regulation as commodity pools.

As a general matter, fund directors should be satisfied that a fund has procedures in place to ensure compliance with applicable provisions of the CEA and the CFTC's regulations, including (i) compliance with the conditions of Rule 4.5 for funds that have claimed Rule 4.5 relief and (ii) compliance with applicable CFTC requirements for funds that are not eligible for such relief. Fund directors should also be satisfied that the fund's adviser and/or sub-adviser has the appropriate CFTC registrations (or is eligible for and has claimed an exemption from registration), and that the advisers are otherwise in compliance with applicable CEA requirements and the CFTC's rules for CTAs.

E. Other Regulators

Regulators other than the SEC and the CFTC have scrutinized and taken action with respect to the activities of funds, fund directors, fund advisers and distributors and other service providers. FINRA, which regulates many of the intermediaries that sell fund shares, has been active in the sales practice and revenue sharing areas and this will likely continue as fund practices for the sale of fund shares evolve. State authorities have also brought civil and criminal charges involving funds.

F. Impact of the Dodd-Frank Act

While fund net asset values were hit hard by the 2008–2009 financial crisis, and one money market fund "broke the buck" after the Lehman bankruptcy, funds fared considerably better as a group than other institutions, such as hedge funds, banks, and securities firms. As a consequence, the core provisions of the Dodd-Frank Act focus, for the most part, on areas of the financial services industry other than the fund sector. These provisions of the Dodd-Frank Act are primarily intended to prevent the recurrence of events causing the financial crisis and lower risk in the U.S. financial system. While the Act generally does not apply to funds directly, funds do enter into transactions with financial institutions and other entities directly impacted by the Dodd-Frank Act and invest in securities issued or underwritten by such entities. Accordingly, for many funds, the Dodd-Frank Act's biggest impact has been, and will likely continue to be, on the structure and liquidity of the securities and derivatives markets in which the funds trade. It should be noted that a number of regulations required by the Dodd-Frank Act have not yet been adopted as of the date of publication, the compliance dates for others vary, and that it is possible that some of the compliance deadlines may be extended. The following are among the more noteworthy provisions that are relevant to funds.

The Dodd-Frank Act's Section 619, otherwise known as the "Volcker Rule," prohibits proprietary trading (and other high-risk trading strategies) by banking entities and their affiliates (with certain exceptions). The Volcker Rule may increase market fragmentation, which could limit funds' ability to execute trades in certain markets, especially in times of high volatility.

The Dodd-Frank Act's Title VII is another area of potential impact on funds. This section mandates a comprehensive regulatory transformation of the United States' over-the-counter and security-based swap markets and market participants thereon. Statutory requirements include mandatory central clearing, recordkeeping, and reporting of swap transaction data; mandatory capital and margin requirements for uncleared swaps; and position limits for certain market participants on particular agricultural, energy, and metals swap transactions. At this point, it is unclear whether these changes will have a material effect on the economics of the transactions and on certain investment strategies more generally.

The Dodd-Frank Act also established a new type of framework for governing and regulating credit rating agencies, including nationally recognized statistical rating organizations ("NRSROs"). As required by the Dodd-Frank Act, the SEC has been reviewing its rules and in many cases deleting references to ratings, which arguably increases directors' responsibilities in respect of their oversight of credit quality as there is now greater emphasis on independent credit evaluations by fund advisers. For those funds that are active in the municipal markets, the Dodd-Frank Act requires NRSROs to apply consistent rating standards for all types of securities, including municipal and corporate bonds. These new standards may enable some funds to participate more actively in the market, but may also result in additional margin requirements for certain municipal securities that were financed as a result of lowered ratings.

The Dodd-Frank Act imposes additional regulation on short selling of securities by amending the 1934 Act to prohibit any "manipulative short sale of any security," while requiring the SEC to issue rules mandating public disclosure at least monthly of short sale activity in each security. This requirement may improve stock market transparency and allow fund managers to identify stocks at greater risk for a short squeeze.

Additionally, the Dodd-Frank Act required the SEC to promulgate new rules designed to increase the transparency of information available with respect to the lending or borrowing of securities and with respect to the underlying assets that comprise asset-backed securities. These rules should benefit funds that participate in securities lending and asset-backed securities investing, respectively.

Finally, the Dodd-Frank Act created the Financial Stability Oversight Council ("FSOC"), which has the power to designate non-banks as "systemically important," and has been considering whether it would be appropriate for them to so designate some asset managers or funds. Designation would subject the asset managers or funds to enhanced prudential standards and supervision by the Board of Governors of the Federal Reserve System, in addition to the SEC regulation to which they are already subject. This additional regulation, which would include statutorily mandated requirements in areas including risk management, capital, leverage, liquidity, and stress testing, would be implemented on a consolidated basis and would likely be tailored to each designated asset manager or fund. As a result, designation could have a significant impact on designated entities and the asset management industry more broadly.

As the regulatory implementation of Dodd-Frank progresses, directors should stay apprised of developments for potential impact on the funds they oversee.

G. Development of Best Practices

For many years, industry-related groups have been developing guides for fund directors and formulating "best practices." Initially published in 1996, the Guidebook was the first well-known guide for fund directors.

In 1999 an advisory group of fund directors and industry executives formed by the Investment Company Institute ("ICI") and published a report (the "ICI Best Practices Report") identifying a variety of practices beyond those required by law for investment company boards and independent directors to consider adopting. In July 2004, the Mutual Fund Directors Forum ("MFDF") published a "best practices" report providing practical guidance regarding board review of management arrangements and other fund-related matters. That MFDF report was updated in 2013. The MFDF and the Independent Directors Council ("IDC"), which is affiliated with the ICI, have each published reports on specific topics that have included, among others: soft dollars, board self-assessments, Rule 12b-1, board oversight of multiple funds, valuation, subadvisers, risk management, proxy voting, securities lending, intermediary relationships, fund mergers, service providers, investment performance, target date funds, alternative investments, the board/CCO relationship, and annual evaluation by the audit committee of the independent auditors. Many fund directors find these recommendations and reports to provide useful benchmarks and guidance, although they are generally not intended to be prescriptive. For example the MFDF's 2004 report states that "the diversity among funds and fund families means it is not possible to develop a 'one-size-fits-all' set of best practices" and noted that its recommendations "may not be appropriate for every fund or fund family, or even for each fund in a family in all instances."

H. Importance of Staying Current with Industry and Regulatory Developments

The manner and the environment in which funds operate are constantly evolving, as are the regulations governing fund and investment management activities. It is essential that fund management and directors (not to mention the chief compliance officers of the fund and its service providers) stay abreast of new industry and regulatory developments affecting how business is conducted.

Fiduciary Duties and Responsibilities of Fund Directors

A. Responsibilities and Duties of Fund Directors Under State Law

1) Introduction

Fund directors, like directors of operating companies, have two basic functions under state law: oversight and decision making. Oversight has two separate, though overlapping, features for fund directors: overseeing compliance with the fund's statutory and regulatory requirements and overseeing the fund's relationship with its investment adviser (and affiliates of the adviser) and other service providers. Effective oversight generally requires regular attention to systems, controls, policy issues, and other recurring matters as well as attention to matters suggesting a need for further inquiry. The second function, decision making, includes both matters as to which the law requires board action (such as the election of officers, dividend authorization, approval of charter amendments and mergers) and other matters where board approval is good corporate practice (such as borrowing or initiation of or a response to major litigation). Unlike operating companies, however, where directors are often called upon to make decisions affecting the company's core business, decision making for a fund's core business—the buying and selling of securities for the fund's investment portfolio—is usually vested with the investment adviser. Fund directors, compared to corporate directors, may be called upon to devote a greater portion of their time on oversight of regulatory compliance and the investment adviser's compliance with fiduciary duties.

In furtherance of their oversight and decision-making functions, fund directors perform various tasks, such as (i) reviewing and approving fundamental operating, financial, and governance policies relevant to the fund; (ii) evaluating fund performance and taking appropriate action where necessary, including potentially renegotiating the terms of the management agreement and, in the most extreme cases, nonrenewal or termination of the management agreement; (iii) reviewing and approving investment management fees; (iv) reviewing procedures for providing financial and operational information to the board; (v) changing the size of the board; (vi) nominating directors and filling board vacancies; (vii) appointing and operating committees of the board; (viii) approving the issuance of shares; (ix) authorizing dividends and share repurchases; (x) calling regular or special shareholder meetings; (xi) electing officers and appointing agents; and (xii) reviewing, and considering approval of, major transactions, including fund mergers and liquidations.

In performing their oversight and decision-making functions, directors have various individual and collective duties and responsibilities. In some states, a director's duties may be prescribed by statute—for example, in Maryland, a director must act (i) in good faith; (ii) with a reasonable belief that the director's action is in the best interests of the corporation; and (iii) with the care of an ordinarily prudent person in a like position under similar circumstances. In many states, however, the primary duties of a director under state law are generally characterized as a duty of loyalty and a duty of care developed through case law. The duties of loyalty and care are often referred to as a director's "fiduciary duties," but the term "fiduciary," when used in the corporate context, does not have the same meaning or attributes as in the law of trusts and may vary from state to state. It should also be noted that, in addition to state laws regarding the duties of a director, the 1940 Act empowers the SEC to bring an action in federal court against a director of a registered investment company for "a breach of fiduciary duty involving personal misconduct," effectively imposing an overarching fiduciary standard on a fund director. All directors should thus be familiar with the duties of loyalty and care, even where state law imposes different duties on a director.

2) Duty of Loyalty

The duty of loyalty requires a director to act in good faith and in the best interests of the fund—and not in the director's own interests or in the interests of another person (e.g., a family member) or organization with which the director is associated or in some way that is reasonably likely to call into question whether the director's action is in the fund's best interests. Simply put, a director must not use his position for personal profit, gain, or other personal advantage. Where a director has a direct or personal interest in a transaction involving the fund, the director must take particular precaution to avoid improper self-dealing and to satisfy the applicable legal requirements, which usually include at least disclosure. Most state corporation statutes, as well as laws applicable to business trusts, prescribe conditions or procedures for authorization, approval, or ratification of interested director transactions in order to insulate such transactions from being void or voidable solely by reason of the conflict.

(a) Acting in Good Faith

The fundamental requirement of loyalty is that a director must act with a good faith reasonable belief that his actions are in the best interests of the fund. A director fails to act in good faith when the director intentionally or knowingly disregards his duties or responsibilities. A director may fail to act in good faith in a variety of ways, including intentionally acting with a purpose other than advancing the fund's best interests; failing to act when there is a known duty to act; acting with the intent to violate, or with intentional disregard of, an applicable law; intentionally disclosing confidential information about the fund; taking for himself or herself a corporate opportunity that could otherwise benefit the fund; or failing to respond to obvious red flags.

(b) Avoiding Conflicts of Interest

Conflicting interest transactions are sometimes unavoidable and are not inherently improper. When a director has a direct or indirect financial or personal interest in a matter before the board for decision—such as a transaction to which the fund is to be a party and in which the director may have an interest—the director is considered under state law to be "interested" in the matter. This status under state law is distinct from the concept of an "interested person" as defined in the 1940 Act, and it triggers specific legal duties under state law.

State statutes usually provide specific procedures for authorizing or ratifying interested director transactions. Typically, either the disinterested directors (or a committee of disinterested directors) or the disinterested shareholders, with full disclosure of material information about the transaction, may authorize or ratify the transaction. Following one of these two "safe harbors" protects both the fund and any interested director from liability and protects the validity and enforceability of any action taken. If one of these two "safe harbors" is not followed and the transaction is challenged, then the interested director has the burden of proving the fairness (and, in Maryland, the reasonableness) of the transaction to the fund, judged according to the circumstances at the time of commitment.

A director, even after disclosing a conflict of interest to fellow directors, should generally abstain from voting on matters in which he or she has a conflict of interest. In most situations, after disclosing the interest, describing the relevant facts, and responding to any questions, the interested director should leave the meeting while the disinterested directors complete their deliberations. This enables the disinterested directors to discuss the matter without being (or creating the appearance of being) influenced by the presence of the interested director. Disclosures of conflicts of interest and the results of the disinterested directors' consideration of the matter should be appropriately documented in minutes or reports. In some cases, creation of a special committee of disinterested directors to review and pass on the transaction may be appropriate.

Disinterested directors reviewing an interested-director transaction should seek to determine (i) whether the terms of the proposed transaction are at least as favorable to the fund as might be available from unrelated persons or entities and (ii) whether the proposed transaction is reasonably likely to further the fund's objectives or otherwise be in the fund's best interests.

(c) Independent Advice

Independent advice regarding the scope and application of the duty of loyalty and the treatment of a conflict of interest or related person transaction is generally helpful in enabling directors to reach informed decisions. This advice may be contained (i) in oral or written opinions or in valuations by financial advisers or appraisers; (ii) in legal advice or opinions on various issues; or (iii) in analyses, reports or recommendations by other relevant experts.

3) Duty of Care

In Delaware, where many funds are organized, and in states that have adopted the Model Business Corporation Act (the "Model Act"), a director who acts with the care that an ordinarily prudent person in a like position would reasonably believe appropriate under similar circumstances has met the director's duty of care to the fund. The duty of care includes the following:

(a) Need to be Informed and Prepared

A director's duty of care primarily relates to the responsibility to become and remain reasonably informed in overseeing the fund's activities and in making decisions. Compliance with the duty of care under state law is based upon diligence applied to the needs of the fund, including obtaining and reviewing adequate information (including the advice of experts, as appropriate), deliberating carefully, avoiding undue haste, making appropriate inquiries as required under particular circumstances, and regularly attending and participating in board and committee meetings. When contemplating specific actions, a director should receive the relevant information in sufficient time to be able to study and reflect on the materials and the issues presented. If a director believes that information is insufficient or inaccurate, or is not made available in a timely manner, the director should request additional information and a delay of the decision until appropriate information is available and can be studied. If a director believes that expert advice would be helpful in exercising oversight or in making a decision, the director should request it.

(b) Right to Rely on Others

A director generally is entitled to rely on reports, opinions, information, and statements (including financial statements and other financial data) presented by the fund's officers or employees, its investment adviser, administrator, or distributor so long as the director reasonably believes those who have prepared or presented the information to be reliable and competent in the matters covered. A director may similarly rely on legal counsel, independent public accountants, and other persons as to matters that the director reasonably believes to be within their professional or expert competence. A director may also rely on a board committee on which the director does not serve as to a matter within its power if the director reasonably believes that the committee merits confidence. However, the right to rely does not mean that a director should defer without further exercise of his duties. In addition, the right to rely does not protect a director who has information concerning the matter in question that would cause reliance to be unwarranted (see Section 4.B).

(c) Inquiry

In overseeing the investment adviser, a director should bear in mind that conflicts of interest are inherent where the investment adviser manages money on behalf of multiple clients and in the external management structure of the fund itself. Directors should oversee the investment adviser's performance and also its trading practices, including the manner in which the investment adviser seeks best execution when trading the fund's portfolio securities.

A director should inquire into any potential problems or issues when alerted to circumstances or events suggesting that board attention is appropriate. For example, inquiry is warranted when information appears materially inaccurate or inadequate; when there is reason to question the competence, loyalty or candor of the fund's officers or employees, investment adviser, administrator, distributor, or other service provider; or when common sense raises questions under the circumstances. When a director has information indicating that the fund is or may be experiencing significant problems or engaging in potentially unlawful conduct, the director should promptly make further inquiry and follow up until reasonably satisfied that the situation is being addressed appropriately. Even when there are no obvious "red flags," directors should satisfy themselves periodically that the fund maintains systems and procedures that are appropriately designed to identify and manage compliance and investment risks and are reasonably effective in maintaining compliance with laws and fund policies and procedures.

(d) Time Commitment and Regular Attendance

A director should commit the required time to prepare for, regularly attend, and participate in board and committee meetings. Many states allow for participation to take place by telephone or other means of communication by which all directors can hear each other, but directors who are physically present at a meeting also have the opportunity to engage in spontaneous interactions that occur before, during, and after the meeting and are often more aware of the group's dynamics. (See Section 4.C(3) for further discussion of a director's expected time commitment and Section 4.C(4) for further discussion of the 1940 Act requirement that certain matters be approved at an in-person meeting.)

(e) Deliberation

Candid discussion among directors and between directors and management is important. In both board and committee meetings, directors should deliberate collectively as a board, asking questions, expressing their views and listening to the views of the other directors and of management. A director should question information provided by management, advisers, or others if the director feels, based on individual knowledge and experience, that such information may be inaccurate or incomplete. Directors should avoid haste. If a director feels more time is needed to consider a matter, the director should ask for it and, within reason, considering the circumstances, should be allowed additional time.

(f) Disclosure Among Directors

Each director should disclose to other directors information known to the director to be significant to the oversight or decision-making responsibilities of the board or its committees. Directors occasionally have legal or other duties of confidentiality owed to another corporation or entity. When such a situation arises, a director should seek legal advice regarding the director's obligations, which ordinarily would include reporting to the other directors the existence of the confidentiality obligations and not participating in consideration of the matter.

4) *Other Duties*

In addition to liability for breach of the duties of care or loyalty, state law may impose liability on a director for specific actions, such as authorizing unlawful dividends or other distributions or authorizing violations of the fund's governing instrument. A director may also be subject to personal liability under other state laws. Proper oversight and careful monitoring of fund and service provider programs directed toward legal compliance should provide substantial safeguards against personal liability.

B. Fund Directors' Responsibilities Under the 1940 Act

In addition to statutory and common law obligations, fund directors are also subject to specific fiduciary obligations relating to the special nature of funds under the 1940 Act. To protect fund shareholders, the 1940 Act requires that each registered fund be governed by a board of directors. The Act further requires that at least 40% of a fund's board be independent in order to serve as "independent watchdogs" in monitoring the fund's managing organizations. Higher percentages of independent directors are common in practice and a majority of a fund's directors must be independent in order for the fund to rely on certain exemptive rules that most funds rely upon. A fund board has the responsibility, among other duties, to monitor the conflicts of interest facing the fund's investment adviser and determine how the conflicts should be managed to help ensure that the fund is being operated in the best interest of the fund's shareholders (see Section 7.A(2)).

Fund Governance

A. Composition of the Board—The Independent Director

1) Desirability of Independent Directors Generally

The 1940 Act contemplates independent oversight and monitoring of investment company operations. The interests of the investment company and its shareholders are of undivided concern only to the independent directors. Their status as other than "interested persons" is intended to permit them to act with genuine independence in addressing conflict-of-interest situations.

Mistakes made by a fund's adviser or other service providers, including violations of fund policies or applicable laws and trading and processing errors occur from time to time. Given the nature of fund operations, the consequences of violations or errors may be significant. The independent directors should receive reports concerning these matters and be satisfied with the corrective actions taken in response, which will often be pursuant to the fund's or service provider's compliance policies and procedures previously approved by the board. In appropriate cases the independent directors may determine to involve independent experts and negotiate a resolution with management or the relevant service providers. In all cases the independent directors must exercise independent judgment in seeking a resolution that is appropriate and in the best interests of the fund in light of the relevant facts and circumstances.

2) 1940 Act Independence Requirements

Section 10(a) of the 1940 Act provides generally that at least 40% of the members of an investment company's board of directors must be independent, meaning that they not be an "interested person" of the fund, as defined in the 1940 Act. In 2001, the SEC adopted a special set of governance standards (the "SEC Governance Standards") contained in Rule 0-1(a)(7) that serve as conditions to a number of exemptive rules adopted by the SEC including Rule 12b-1 (permitting use of fund assets to pay distribution expenses) and rules that permit funds to engage in certain types of transactions with affiliates. Each of the exemptive rules contains the condition that the board of directors of the fund must satisfy the SEC Governance Standards. As a practical matter, the SEC Governance Standards apply to most funds because few funds can operate without having the ability to rely upon one or more of the exemptive rules conditioned on compliance with the standards. The SEC Governance Standards require that a majority of the directors be independent. The boards of most funds have been in compliance with this standard for many years. The ICI best practices report recommends that at least two-thirds of an investment company's board members be independent and the MFDF report recommends that at least 75% be independent.

In 2004, the SEC adopted amendments to the SEC Governance Standards that would have required an investment company board to have at least 75% independent directors (66% in the case of a three-member board) and for the board's chair to be an independent director. The U.S. Chamber of Commerce initiated a number of legal challenges to these requirements, and a federal appeals court ultimately invalidated them. In 2006, the SEC sought additional comment on the requirements, but has not taken further action. Thus, there is no legal requirement for 75% independent director membership on a fund board.

The term "interested person" is defined in Section 2(a)(19) of the 1940 Act. This important definition is highly technical in nature and must be approached with great care. It includes (i) certain categories of persons with interests potentially in conflict with the investment company, (ii) persons with any beneficial or legal interest in securities issued by the investment adviser or principal underwriter or their control persons, (iii) brokers or dealers that effect portfolio transactions on behalf of or with the investment company or certain related entities within the last six months, (iv) persons loaning money or other property to the investment company or certain related entities, and (v) a person or partner or employee of a person who within the last two years has served as legal counsel for the investment company or its investment adviser or principal underwriter. The term "interested person" also encompasses persons with close familial, substantial financial, or certain professional relationships with an "affiliated person" of the investment company, including its investment adviser. A person who has been convicted of certain securities laws violations, enjoined from engaging in certain securities-related activities or prohibited by the SEC or by court order from serving as a director because of willful violations of the securities laws is ineligible to serve as a fund director.

Boards sometimes are faced with the question of whether a former officer or director of a fund's investment adviser or principal underwriter can serve as an independent director of a fund. Section 2(a)(19) provides that the SEC by order may determine a person is an "interested person" by reason of having had a material business or professional relationship with the fund's adviser or underwriter or with the principal executive officer or any controlling person of the adviser or underwriter of the fund within the last two fiscal years. As a result, boards that want to consider a former officer or director of the adviser or underwriter for an independent director position often choose to deem such individual "interested" for at least two full fiscal years and may re-consider the question at the end of that period. The ICI best practices report goes even further and recommends that former officers or directors of an investment company's investment adviser, principal underwriter or related entities not serve as independent directors. The MFDF best practices report recommends that such persons not serve as independent directors if they have been affiliated with the fund's adviser or its affiliates within the last five years. In addition, SEC rules require public disclosures about independent directors, including information that could potentially raise conflict-of-interest concerns. Consequently, it is important that the status and relationships of a potential director be considered carefully by counsel prior to his joining the board.

Generally, fund shareholders elect directors in accordance with state law and the SEC's proxy solicitation rules. Many open-end funds, ETFs, and unlisted closed-end funds are not required under applicable state law to hold annual meetings of shareholders. In Maryland, where many open-end funds are incorporated, a fund's charter or bylaws may eliminate the need for an annual meeting of shareholders in any year in which election of directors is not required under the 1940 Act. Funds organized as trusts, which are governed by their declarations of trust, also are generally not required to hold annual shareholder meetings. Closed-end funds with securities listed on an exchange are required to have annual shareholder meetings (see Section 13.A(3)). Under the 1940 Act, vacancies on a board generally may be filled by the directors (without a shareholder vote) if, after the new director takes office, at least two-thirds of the board has been elected by shareholders. If the number of shareholder-elected board members decreases to less than half of the board, a fund must hold a shareholder meeting for the purpose of electing directors within 60 days.

3) Independent Chair

As noted above, in 2001 the SEC amended the SEC Governance Standards to require that chairs of fund boards be independent, but this requirement was invalidated after a court challenge. Thus, there is no legal requirement for fund boards to have an independent chair.

Where there is no board chair or the role of chair is filled by a "management" director, the independent directors may consider designating one of their members to act as a lead independent director. This director can serve as the focal point for governance and operational practices enhancing the role of the independent directors, including other matters related to the requirements of the Sarbanes-Oxley Act and the SEC Governance Standards. The SEC requires a fund to disclose whether the board chair is independent, and where such person is not independent, the fund must disclose whether it has a lead independent director and what specific role the lead independent director plays in the leadership of the fund.

4) Importance of Maintaining Independence

The consequences of failing to maintain the requisite number of independent directors required by Section 10(a) of the 1940 Act or by the SEC Governance Standards can be severe. The 1940 Act requires that certain matters and contractual arrangements—including the advisory and distribution arrangements—be approved by a majority of independent directors. An investment advisory agreement approved by an improperly constituted board under Section 10(a) of the 1940 Act may not be valid, and, among other things, the adviser may be required to return fees received under the contract or provide its services at cost. Similarly, funds that do not satisfy the SEC Governance Standards, which include that a majority of the directors be independent, are not able to rely upon any of the exemptive rules conditioned on compliance with such standards. For example, payments made by a fund to its distributor or underwriter under a Rule 12b-1 distribution plan that has not been approved by a properly constituted board may be recoverable by the fund. To the extent the requisite number of independent directors has not been maintained, other board actions may be subject to challenge as well.

Changes in outside affiliations of independent directors, changes in the adviser's ownership structure, or the addition of new sub-advisers should be monitored to help ensure that an independent director does not inadvertently become an interested person of the fund or become otherwise disqualified. It is common practice for independent directors to complete, on an annual basis, a questionnaire on business, financial, and family relationships, if any, with the adviser, principal underwriter, other service providers, and their affiliates. If a questionnaire is used, it is important that the responses be reviewed carefully by counsel or compliance personnel.

5) Service on More Than One Board in a Complex

It has long been industry practice for fund boards to include directors who serve on more than one board in a fund complex. For complexes with a large number of funds, this is a practical necessity. Although there are areas of common interest among the funds, the directors must exercise their specific board responsibilities on a fund-by-fund basis. Broadened exposure to the operations of a complex can be valuable to a board member and provide a better context for carrying out board functions, such as serving the independent directors' "watchdog" role. Service on multiple boards also facilitates administrative convenience.

The SEC has taken the position that service on multiple boards of the same fund complex does not make a director an "interested person" under the 1940 Act. The laws of Maryland and certain other states provide that a director who is not an "interested person" under the 1940 Act shall be presumed to be independent under state law. The ICI best practices report recommends that investment company boards of directors generally be organized either as a unitary board for all the funds in a complex or as cluster boards for groups of funds within a complex, rather than as separate boards for each individual fund. There has been litigation challenging the independence of directors who serve on multiple boards of funds within the same fund complex. None of these challenges has been successful to date.

The SEC Governance Standards require that the board of directors evaluate, at least annually, the performance of the board. This annual self-assessment must include a consideration of, among other things, the number of funds on whose boards each director serves. (For a more in-depth discussion of the self-assessment requirement, see Section 4.C(7)).

B. Board Committees

Boards of investment companies often find it useful to appoint committees of the board to which specified functions and responsibilities are delegated. The board must have an audit committee and frequently has other committees, such as contracts, performance, compliance, or nominating committees, among others. Other special or *ad hoc* committees may be established for special purposes such as to investigate allegations of wrongdoing, or a pricing or valuation problem, or in connection with a governmental investigation or unusual conflict situations. The Guidebook does not address these special situations. Also not addressed are the difficult issues faced by special litigation committees appointed to determine the proper course of action to take when derivative litigation is brought against directors.

Where specific responsibilities are legally assigned to the full board or to the independent directors, the board may ask a committee to consider these matters preliminarily and to make recommendations to the full board (or to the independent directors). If action is required to be taken by the independent directors only, any committee to which the matter is assigned for preliminary consideration should consist solely of independent directors. The full board (or the independent directors), however, must act upon matters where there is a legal obligation to do so and will bear full responsibility for the action taken. In other instances, a director who is not a member of a committee may generally rely upon committee action under state law if (i) the composition of the committee is appropriate for its purpose and the committee has been properly constituted, (ii) the full board makes reasonable efforts to keep abreast of the activities of the committee and is kept informed of committee activities, and (iii) the committee acts within the limits of its authority under applicable law and charter provisions.

1) Audit Committees

The Sarbanes-Oxley Act and exchange rules adopted pursuant thereto impose requirements for the audit committees of listed closed-end funds and ETFs in terms of its composition and its role and authority. The Sarbanes-Oxley Act requirements do not, however, supplant or lessen the importance of the 1940 Act requirements as to director independence and the extensive role of independent directors in the regulatory regime of the 1940 Act.

(a) Composition of the Audit Committee

The listing requirements of national securities exchanges provide that each member of the fund's audit committee must be independent according to specified criteria that are different from those under the 1940 Act (see Section 13.G(1)). The listing requirements are directly applicable only to closed-end funds with listed securities and to ETFs, but may serve as a "best practices" guide for open-end funds.

There are no required qualifications for service on an audit committee under the 1940 Act. Open- and closed-end funds must, however, identify in their annual reports filed with the SEC at least one audit committee member that the board of directors has determined to be an "audit committee financial expert" ("ACFE") as defined by SEC rule. If such a fund does not have an ACFE serving on its audit committee, it must so disclose in the annual report and explain why it does not. If the fund has more than one ACFE, it may, but it is not required to, disclose more than one name. To determine whether a person is an ACFE, the board of directors must find that the person possesses specified attributes and has acquired such attributes through a broad range of specified types of professional experience. The board decision as to whether someone is an ACFE for these purposes and the decision as to the number to be named in the annual report should be made in a considered manner with the help of counsel.

The primary benefit of having an ACFE serve on the audit committee, according to the SEC, is to provide a resource for the audit committee as a whole in carrying out its functions. The SEC provides a safe harbor provision in the audit committee disclosure item (Item 3(d) of Form N-CSR) for the ACFE under federal securities (but not necessarily state) law:

- A person who is determined to be an ACFE will not be deemed an "expert" for any purpose, including without limitation for purposes of Section 11 of the 1933 Act, as a result of being designated or identified as an ACFE pursuant to the disclosure item; and
- The designation or identification of a person as an ACFE pursuant to the disclosure item does not impose on such person any duties, obligations or liabilities that are greater than the duties, obligations and liability imposed on such person as a member of the audit committee and board of directors in the absence of such designation or identification.

The SEC has stated that the designation or identification of a person as an ACFE does not affect the duties, obligations or liability of any other member of the audit committee or board of directors.

(b) Role and Authority of the Audit Committee

An audit committee generally oversees a fund's relationship with its auditors and acts as a liaison between the independent auditors and the full board. The audit committee oversees the accounting and financial reporting processes of the fund, the quality and integrity of the fund's financial statements and the independent audit of the fund's financial statements. The audit committee also oversees the fund's compliance with the legal and regulatory requirements that relate to the fund's internal control over financial reporting.

The Sarbanes-Oxley Act and SEC exchange rules adopted pursuant thereto impose various requirements for audit committees in terms of their role and authority. The listing requirements provide that the audit committee is directly responsible for the appointment, compensation, retention and oversight of the auditors. The audit committee is authorized to evaluate and, if necessary, terminate the auditors. In addition, Section 32(a) of the 1940 Act provides that independent auditors of registered investment companies must be selected for each fiscal year by a majority vote of the independent directors (see Section 7.C(3)). In connection with the annual approval of the audit engagement, the audit committee must receive information from the auditors to enable the committee to evaluate the auditors' independence.

A fund's independent auditors are required to submit an annual report to the audit committee that must include (i) all critical accounting policies and practices used and disclose all alternative treatments of financial information within generally accepted accounting principles that have been discussed with management, (ii) the ramifications of such alternative treatments and (iii) the auditors' preferred course. The auditors must also report any accounting disagreements between the auditors and management.

The audit committee should meet periodically with the auditors, without the participation of management, to review the reports of the auditors. In this setting, the auditors typically are asked whether there are any matters regarding the fund, its financial reporting and recordkeeping, and its operations that make the auditors uncomfortable; whether adequate accounting systems and controls are in place; whether management has adequate staffing; and whether there is any weakness in systems and controls that needs strengthening and, if so, the auditors' recommendations as to such strengthening.

Because of concern that management consulting services offered by accounting firms created substantial conflicts that eroded the independence of auditors, the Sarbanes-Oxley Act and the SEC's auditor independence rules mandated thereby specify a number of non-audit services that auditors cannot provide to their clients, such as financial information systems design and implementation, bookkeeping, and other services related to the accounting records or financial statements. The auditors also may not provide a variety of other non-audit services, such as internal audit outsourcing, legal services, and investment advisory services.

Auditors may perform non-audit services (including certain types of tax services) that are not on the prohibited list for an audit client only if the audit committee approves the activity in advance. Preapproval by the audit committee is also required for permissible non-audit services provided to the fund's investment adviser, and any entity controlling, controlled by, or under common control with the investment adviser that provides ongoing services to the fund, if the engagement relates directly to the operations and financial reporting of the fund. The audit committee is not required to preapprove audit or non-audit services provided to an unaffiliated sub-adviser that primarily provides portfolio management services to the fund. The audit committee may delegate the authority to preapprove non-audit services to one or more members of the audit committee. Audit committee approval of non-audit services must be disclosed in the periodic reports filed with the SEC.

The SEC auditor independence and audit committee pre-approval rules include provisions that treat services by auditors to other members of a fund's investment company complex the same as services to the fund in many cases.

The lead partner and reviewing audit partners on the audit team are subject to a five-year rotation requirement. There is a one-year cooling-off period for anyone on the audit team who seeks to be employed in a senior financial management capacity with respect to the fund.

Fund directors should be aware that business or consulting relationships a director has with a fund's auditors or the auditors' affiliates may compromise the auditors' independence. In 2015, the SEC brought an enforcement action against an audit firm based on the SEC's finding that the audit firm had violated auditor independence rules when its consulting affiliate maintained a business relationship with a director serving on the boards and audit committees of funds it audited. The SEC also charged the independent director on the basis that he had caused related reporting violations by the funds, and charged the funds' administrator with causing related compliance violations.

It is unlawful for any officer or director, or person acting under his direction, to improperly influence the auditors for the purpose of rendering the financial statements materially misleading. The SEC rules provide that, in the case of funds, persons acting under the direction of officers and directors of the fund may include, among others, officers, directors, and employees of the investment adviser, sponsor, distributor or other service providers. The SEC has stated that conduct it believes might constitute improper influence includes (i) threatening to cancel or canceling existing non-audit or audit engagements if the auditors object to the fund's accounting and (ii) seeking to have a partner removed from the audit engagement because the partner objects to the fund's accounting. The independent directors must take care to avoid engaging in conduct with respect to the auditors that could be construed as improper influence. In their discussions with the auditors, the audit committee should make inquiries as to whether anyone has tried to improperly influence the auditors.

It is unlawful for a fund to retaliate against an employee or "agent" who has provided information about possible fraud or violations of federal law to enforcement authorities and others (so-called whistleblower protection). The listing requirements provide that the audit committee must establish procedures for handling complaints and for confidential, anonymous submissions by employees regarding accounting/auditing matters and such procedures are a best practice for all funds (see Section 7.C(11)).

Fund auditors also typically report to the audit committee on whether the audit firm has been reviewed by the Public Company Accounting Oversight Board ("PCAOB") and the results of that review, including whether the fund audits were specifically reviewed by the PCAOB or whether other issues were raised by the PCAOB regarding the audit firm's controls that are relevant to a fund's audit.

2) Nominating Committees

To help ensure director independence, the SEC Governance Standards require independent directors to select and nominate other independent directors. The SEC Governance Standards do not mandate a committee in this regard. If there is a nominating committee, it should be properly structured, with a designated chair and with procedures designed to ensure that, as a matter of appearance as well as reality, the selection of nominees is made by the nominating committee.

The investment adviser may play an appropriate role in the selection and recommendation of candidates for election to the fund's board. The adviser has a legitimate interest in ensuring, for example, that the independent directors are qualified and are not unduly associated with competitors. On the other hand, the adviser should not be permitted to participate in the process in a manner that limits the independent directors' discretion.

3) Other Committees

Other standing committees are sometimes created by fund boards to focus on specific areas. Thus, a board may have, for example, pricing or valuation, contracts, regulatory compliance, brokerage, and governance committees. In each case, the purpose is to designate an appropriate number of directors as a committee to devote time to the particular matter under review and make recommendations to the board. For example, a pricing committee may review the criteria used by a fund to determine when to use fair value pricing and review the methodology used in valuing portfolio securities for which market quotations are not readily available (see Section 8). A governance committee might be charged with responsibility for developing, recommending, and evaluating a set of corporate governance principles applicable to the fund and procedures for conducting performance evaluations of the board.

C. Board Operations

1) Operating Style

Boards of directors should conduct their proceedings in a manner calculated to encourage, reinforce, and demonstrate the board's role in providing independent oversight of the fund's affairs and the performance of its investment adviser. Board practice will, over time, significantly affect the extent to which a board of directors is likely to discharge its obligations in a manner that effectively protects and advances the interests of the fund's shareholders. No single operational style fits all situations, and there is considerable diversity of practice among fund complexes. A board's operational style may be influenced by many factors, such as the number of funds in the complex, the amount of assets under management, and the fund's distribution methods. Each fund or fund group should develop a style appropriate to its nature and circumstances. Fund directors may find it useful to compare the practices of other fund groups as well as evolving practices in the corporate world. The best practices reports of the ICI and MFDF identify a number of practices followed by fund groups in their governance activities, which may or may not be suitable for every fund board depending upon its individual circumstances.

Independent directors should consider having periodic separate meetings to review the corporate governance policies and standards relating to the manner in which the board conducts its operations. Topics to be considered may include the size of the board and its overall composition, the frequency and length of the meetings, the adequacy of the agendas, the time allotted for the discussion of particular agenda items, the quality of the information being received, the adequacy of access to the personnel of the adviser and others, the adequacy of access to qualified legal counsel sufficiently independent from the adviser and its affiliates, and the adequacy of continuing education as to board members' duties and responsibilities (see Section 4.C(7), which discusses the annual board self-assessment).

2) Size of Board of Directors

There is substantial variation in the size of fund boards. Each fund or fund group should determine optimal board size with a view to ensuring sufficient independent directors to perform the required oversight functions and effective functioning in terms of discussion and decision-making. When directors serve on boards for multiple funds in a complex, factors that might influence board size include the number of funds, the range, diversity and complexity of investment categories, and the complexity of distribution arrangements. If there is concern as to whether the directors can handle the responsibility and workload with respect to the number of funds, the board sizes may be expanded or the complex may add an additional cluster of boards. In accommodating these needs, board size should not be expanded to such an extent as to interfere with effective functioning by making full and free discussion of issues at board meetings impracticable. Larger boards may make increased use of board committees to allocate the workload.

3) Director's Time Commitment

The time commitment expected of directors is a subject that should be reviewed by the board and communicated to existing and prospective directors. Directors should take care not to overcommit themselves, and nominating committees should consider a board candidate's ability to devote the necessary time. <u>Directors should expect to attend, normally in person, all regularly scheduled in-person meetings, and all telephonic meetings as may be regularly scheduled</u> or called from time to time. Disclosure is required in a fund's proxy statement as to those directors who attend fewer than 75% of the aggregate board and committee meetings during the prior full fiscal year. Independent directors are expected to devote sufficient time and attention to the affairs of the fund or fund complex to permit them to prepare for, attend, and participate in meetings of the board and board committees and to keep themselves generally informed about the fund's affairs. The time required varies widely. Fund directors should expect to devote appropriate amounts of time, depending upon the number of meetings and the number and complexity of the funds involved. An independent chair or a lead independent director, and the chair of certain committees including the audit committee, generally will commit substantially more time than other independent directors in light of the greater responsibilities of those positions. In times of crisis, directors will be required to devote additional time.

4) Meetings

It is generally regarded as a "best practice" for directors to be physically present at regular board meetings. Under the 1940 Act, the independent directors are required to meet in person to approve investment advisory and distribution arrangements and the selection of independent auditors. Telephonic and video meetings are generally permissible under applicable state law and may be useful and appropriate for special or emergency meetings. In addition some fund boards and committees find it convenient to schedule regular telephonic meetings of the board or key committees between regularly scheduled in-person board and committee meetings.

The number of meetings a fund board finds necessary or useful varies with the circumstances. Some boards prefer more frequent and shorter meetings. Others prefer fewer but lengthier meetings. In any event, directors should ensure that they have allotted sufficient time for all items to receive sufficient attention. Industry practice ranges from quarterly meetings—generally thought to be the minimum number of meetings necessary for fund directors to discharge their responsibilities properly—to monthly meetings in the case of some larger complexes. Some complexes have quarterly meetings that last two days or more. With the increasing emphasis upon the role of the independent directors, the trend over time has been toward more frequent and longer meetings.

Time at board and committee meetings should be budgeted carefully. There are occasions when the independent directors may wish to—or should—meet without management. The participation of counsel may be desirable to help the independent directors address the issues at hand. In addition, the independent directors may wish to meet informally from time to time to discuss fund matters and generally compare views. The SEC Governance Standards require the independent directors to meet at least once a quarter in executive session and at least once a year in executive session with the fund CCO. Whether a meeting without management is structured as a special committee meeting or as part of a regular board meeting, holding such meetings is an appropriate exercise of independent directors' discretion and a very common fund governance practice.

5) Meeting Agendas

Independent directors should take an active role in determining matters to be discussed and acted upon at board meetings and influencing the priority and amount of time allocated to various matters. In this regard, an independent chair or lead independent director, in consultation with counsel, can play a useful role in coordinating with management. Matters to be discussed and acted upon by the board typically are determined initially by the investment adviser, frequently in consultation with the independent chair or lead independent director or independent counsel to the fund or the independent directors. In any event, independent directors should have an opportunity to place items on the agenda and to influence the priority and amount of time allocated to various matters. A balance should be sought between the investment adviser's presentations and discussion among directors and representatives of the adviser. Directors should be satisfied that there is an annual calendar and agenda that covers all matters that require attention by the board or a committee thereof, such as a review of investment performance, required consideration of the continuance of contract arrangements, required approvals of transactions effected in reliance on exemptive rules, review of other services provided by the adviser and other service providers, and meeting with the independent accountants of the fund.

6) *Independent Counsel and Other Resources*

Independent directors may decide to retain independent legal counsel and other experts, or in some instances to employ their own separate staff, at the fund's expense to assist them in properly performing their responsibilities under the 1940 Act. The SEC Governance Standards require the independent directors to be authorized to hire employees and to retain advisers and experts necessary to carry out their duties. The Sarbanes-Oxley Act listing requirements provide that the audit committee has the authority to engage independent legal counsel and to consult with the fund's independent auditors or other experts, as appropriate, in carrying out its duties and that the issuer must provide appropriate funding for the audit committee as determined by that committee.

The ICI and MFDF best practices reports recommend that independent directors have qualified investment company counsel who is independent from the investment adviser and the fund's other service providers. Whether to retain independent counsel for the independent directors is dependent upon a number of factors. The SEC Governance Standards require that, if counsel is engaged to advise the independent directors, such counsel must be "independent legal counsel" which involves, among other things, a determination by the independent directors at least annually that any representation by such counsel of the fund's investment adviser, principal underwriter, administrator, or any of their control persons, since the beginning of the fund's last two fiscal years, is or was sufficiently limited that it is unlikely to adversely affect the professional judgment of the person in providing legal representation to the independent directors. Counsel that qualifies as "independent legal counsel" often acts both as fund counsel and counsel for the independent directors. In other cases, the relationship of fund counsel to management warrants having the directors consider retaining independent counsel. The size and complexity of a fund group may also warrant retaining independent counsel who can focus upon the needs of the independent directors. In lieu of regular independent counsel, the board might consider engaging independent counsel on an *ad hoc* basis with respect to specific matters.

7) Annual Self-assessments

The SEC Governance Standards require and exchange listing standards may require that fund directors evaluate, at least once annually, the performance of the fund board and its committees. The evaluation is required to include a consideration of the effectiveness of the committee structure of the fund board and the number of funds on whose boards each director serves. The SEC states that this practice is intended to strengthen directors' understanding of their role, foster better communications and greater cohesiveness and help directors identify potential weaknesses and deficiencies in the board's performance. The self-assessment does not have to be in writing, but the SEC expects the board minutes to reflect "the substance of the matters discussed" during an annual self-assessment. Boards use different approaches to conduct the self-assessment, which may include interviews by counsel or completion of a questionnaire by the directors with responses summarized by counsel.

8) Independent Director Compensation

Neither the 1940 Act nor state law sets forth specific requirements or limitations regarding the establishment of directors' compensation. State law generally recognizes that directors are entitled to "reasonable" compensation. The independent directors of a fund, not the adviser, are responsible for setting their own compensation. Because directors have an inherent conflict of interest in determining their compensation, they should seek appropriate data necessary to reach a fair conclusion, including data on comparable funds, together with analysis of any special factors that may relate to the fund or fund group. Independent directors' compensation may take a number of different forms, including annual retainers and attendance fees for board and committee meetings. Deferred compensation plans, retirement programs, and similar benefits are sometimes provided. Independent chairs, lead independent directors, and committee chairs may also receive additional fees and frequently do. The compensation paid to each director by the fund and by the fund complex as a whole must be publicly disclosed in the fund's Statement of Additional Information and proxy statements. Directors who are technically deemed to be "interested persons" but who are not employed by the fund's adviser (or its related entities) also typically receive the same level of compensation as the independent directors.

9) *Procedural Standards Set by the Courts*

Courts have examined the actions of the independent fund directors to determine whether the directors' actions should be upheld in situations involving a conflict of interest between the investment company and the adviser and its affiliates. If proper procedures have been followed, and there has been a valid decision-making process, the courts have been more likely to allow the decision to stand.

Various factors that the courts have cited in assessing the quality of the deliberative process (and, therefore, the weight to be given to director determinations and approvals) include, in no particular order: (i) the relative number of independent directors; (ii) the backgrounds, experience, and expertise of the directors; (iii) the methods utilized in selecting and nominating directors; (iv) the extent to which the directors understand the nature of their statutory duties and responsibilities and are free of domination or undue influence; (v) the extent and quality of the information supplied to the directors by the adviser and the manner in which such information is presented; (vi) the nature of directors' deliberations and whether those deliberations are substantive in nature; (vii) the responsiveness of the adviser to director initiatives seeking additional information or suggesting alternatives to management proposals; and (viii) whether the independent directors have their own independent counsel and have utilized counsel or other qualified experts in reviewing information or considering matters that require special expertise. This is not to say that every factor need be present or has been present in the favorable court decisions.

Independent directors must assure themselves that they have received sufficient information and independent advice to enable them to engage in the requisite deliberations and to support any findings that they are called upon to make. In this regard, both Section 15(c) of the 1940 Act, with respect to investment advisory approvals, and Rule 12b-1, with respect to distribution plan approvals, explicitly impose upon directors the duty to request and evaluate, and make it the duty of the investment adviser or distributor (as the case may be) to furnish such information as may be necessary for the directors to fulfill their duties. Care should be taken to ensure that the minutes of meetings of the board and committees should reflect the factors considered and the basis for the decisions reached.

10) Quality of Information

The quality of information made available to directors significantly impacts their ability to perform their role effectively. To the extent feasible, information submitted to the directors should be relevant, concise, timely, well-organized, supported by any background or historical data necessary or useful to place the information in context, and designed to inform directors of material aspects of a fund's operations, its performance and prospects, and the nature, quality, and cost of the various services provided to the fund by the investment adviser, its affiliates, and other third parties.

Whenever possible, information should be provided in written form sufficiently in advance of the meeting to provide time for thoughtful reflection and meaningful participation by the directors. Many advisers and legal counsel provide directors with annual guidance manuals as to their duties and responsibilities or annual contract review books and regularly apprise directors of recent relevant legal or regulatory developments. The ICI and MFDF best practices reports recommend that new fund directors also receive appropriate orientation and that all fund directors keep abreast of industry and regulatory developments.

Directors should review, and may also ask counsel to review, draft minutes of board and committee meetings before approving them. This task is important as the SEC staff considers the minutes to be evidence of how the directors and the adviser have fulfilled their duties. Board meeting minutes are often requested by the SEC staff and reviewed during SEC inspections and examinations and may also be subject to review in private litigation.

11) Disagreement

Board and committee actions are normally unanimous. However, if a director disagrees with any significant action to be taken by the board, the director may vote against the proposal and may request that the dissent be recorded in the minutes. Under state law, a director is generally presumed to agree unless his dissent is so noted. Except in unusual circumstances, a dissenting vote should not cause a director to consider resigning. If a director believes, however, that information being disclosed by the fund is inadequate, incomplete or incorrect or that the adviser is not dealing with the directors, the shareholders or the public in good faith, the director should seek corrective action and consult with legal counsel (who has no material relationship with the adviser) for purposes of determining an appropriate course of action.

Directors who have a personal interest in a matter being voted on should consider abstaining and, in all events, should disclose their interest. Directors should request that their disclosure and, where relevant, their abstention or withdrawal from the meeting when the relevant matter was discussed, be noted in the board meeting minutes.

12) *Term of Service*

Neither the 1940 Act nor state law sets forth specific requirements on retirement policies or term limits. The ICI best practices report recommends that fund boards adopt policies on retirement of directors. Many boards have adopted a mandatory retirement age policy, typically at ages ranging from 72 to 75. Some boards set a retirement age but allow the board to make an exception for directors with special skills or who make exceptional contributions to the board. Other boards have policies setting term limits that allow directors to serve for a maximum number of years (e.g., 15 years). Some other boards have determined that setting a mandatory retirement age or term limit is not appropriate for their fund or complex.

Board Responsibilities with Respect to Investment Advisory Arrangements

A. Statutory Responsibilities

The 1940 Act contains important provisions governing the relationship between the adviser and the fund's board of directors in considering and approving an advisory contract. Congress viewed these provisions as particularly important given the inherent conflicts of interest between advisers and the funds they manage.

Section 15 of the 1940 Act governs the terms of an advisory contract and the process of entering into, continuing, amending, and terminating the contract. After the initial two-year term, the contract may be continued annually if it is approved either by the full board of directors of the fund or by the shareholders of the fund. Typically, the contract is renewed by the directors, not the shareholders (which is a costly and cumbersome alternative). In addition, any renewal of the advisory contract must separately be approved by a majority of the independent directors at an in-person meeting called for the purpose of voting on the contract.

In entering into or renewing an advisory contract, Section 15(c) provides that it is the duty of the directors to request and evaluate, and the duty of the adviser to furnish, such information as may reasonably be necessary to evaluate the terms of the contract. The advisory agreement for each fund must be considered separately rather than on a complex-wide basis. The annual review of the investment advisory arrangements is commonly called the "15(c) process."

To provide a remedy for excessive compensation, Section 36(b) of the 1940 Act imposes a fiduciary duty upon the adviser with respect to the receipt of compensation for services, or of payments of a material nature, paid by the fund to the adviser or its affiliates. Section 36(b) authorizes actions by shareholders and by the SEC against an adviser (not against fund directors) for breach of this duty.

In *Jones v. Harris Associates L.P.,* a unanimous Supreme Court decision, 130 S. Ct. 1418 (2010), the Court concluded that the Second Circuit's 1982 decision in *Gartenberg v. Merrill Lynch Asset Management, Inc.,* "was correct in its basic formulation of what Section 36(b) requires." In determining whether an adviser has received excessive compensation in breach of its fiduciary duty under Section 36(b), the applicable standard is as follows:

> [T]he essence of the test is whether or not under all the circumstances the transaction carries the earmarks of an arm's length bargain.

> To be guilty of a violation of § 36(b), therefore, the adviser-manager must charge a fee that is so disproportionately large that it bears no reasonable relationship to the services rendered and could not have been the product of arm's-length bargaining. To make this determination, all pertinent facts must be weighed.

The Senate Report accompanying the enactment of Section 36(b) in 1970 states that:

> Nothing in the bill is intended to . . . suggest that a "cost-plus" type of contract would be required. It is not intended to introduce general concepts of rate regulation as applied to public utilities.

B. Factors to Consider in Carrying Out Responsibilities

Section 36(b) directs a court to give approval of the advisory arrangements by the board of directors such consideration as it deems appropriate. The excessive fee cases demonstrate that a valid Section 15(c) approval process is an important factor that increases the likelihood that a contractual advisory fee will be upheld. The excessive fee cases suggest that all of the facts and circumstances surrounding the adviser's relationship with a fund are appropriate for independent director consideration. In determining whether there has been a valid approval process, the *Jones* opinion acknowledges the crucial role of informed and diligent fund directors. According to the Court, "scrutiny of investment adviser compensation by a fully informed mutual fund board is the 'cornerstone of the . . . effort to control conflicts of interest within mutual funds' . . . The Act interposes disinterested directors as 'independent watchdogs' of the relationship between a mutual fund and its adviser." Quoting *Gartenberg*, the Supreme Court further noted that "the expertise of the independent trustees of a fund, whether they are fully informed about all facts bearing on the [investment adviser's] service and fee, and the extent of care and conscientiousness with which they perform their duties are important factors to be considered in deciding whether they and the [investment adviser] are guilty of a breach of fiduciary duty . . ."

Factors the directors often consider include: (i) the nature, extent and quality of the services provided by the investment adviser; (ii) the investment performance of the fund; (iii) the amount and structure of the advisory fee; (iv) the resulting profits realized by the adviser and its affiliates from its relationship with each fund, including the extent to which the adviser has realized economies of scale as a fund grows; and (v) other sources of revenue to the investment adviser and its affiliates from their relationship to the fund and intangible or "fall-out" benefits that accrue to the adviser and its affiliates. These five factors often are referred to as the "Gartenberg factors." This list of factors, however, is not an exhaustive list of all the information boards may wish to consider. Additional information that a board may consider includes: the operating expenses of the fund; the manner in which the portfolio transactions of the fund are conducted, including any use of soft dollars and transactions with affiliates of the adviser; and the entrepreneurial risk and financial exposure assumed in organizing and managing the fund. Experienced counsel can help guide the independent directors through the approval process. In fact, the adviser's delivery of 15(c) materials to the independent directors typically results from a written request made by outside counsel on behalf of the independent directors.

A case brought by the SEC against three independent directors and a fund adviser, Commonwealth Capital Management, LLC, underscores the importance of care at every stage of the 15(c) process, including the board's review of the completeness of information it has requested. The SEC found that the adviser provided incomplete or inaccurate responses to information request letters sent by legal counsel on behalf of the independent directors, but that the boards nevertheless voted to approve the advisory agreements. The SEC noted that, although Section 15(c) does not define what information may be "reasonably necessary" to approve an advisory agreement, that analysis is informed by the "Gartenberg factors."

Courts generally have not "second-guessed" a board's determination as to the fairness of a fee structure if the board has employed appropriate evaluation procedures and has given due consideration to all appropriate factors. In *Jones*, the Supreme Court stressed that "where a board's process for negotiating and reviewing investment-adviser compensation is robust, a reviewing court should afford commensurate deference to the outcome of the bargaining process. If the independent directors considered the relevant factors, their decision to approve a particular fee agreement is entitled to considerable weight, even if a court might weigh the factors differently." Thus, the courts effectively apply a "business judgment rule" in the 1940 Act context.

1) Nature and Quality of the Services

The review of the nature and quality of services provided by an adviser encompasses every service provided to a fund under the advisory agreement. Often, these include compliance and administrative services in addition to portfolio management. In the case of sub-advised funds, these services include selection and oversight of the sub-advisers. Boards typically consider detailed information from the investment adviser about all the services it provides to the funds it manages as part of the 15(c) process.

2) Performance

Fund performance is one of the key measures considered by a board in evaluating the services provided by the investment adviser. Whether the investment adviser employs portfolio managers to invest fund assets or whether it oversees the performance of sub-advisers (see Section 5.D below), boards understand that, for shareholders, performance is a key reason for investing in the fund. As a result, much of a board's focus during the 15(c) process (and, in fact, throughout the year) is on the performance of each of the funds it oversees. Boards frequently compare a fund's performance to its benchmark index. They also often consider the fund's performance relative to that of a similar set of funds. This comparative information, which usually includes funds managed by other investment advisers, often is provided by, or based on information provided by, a third-party data provider. Depending on the type of fund, the relevance of its benchmark index and the comparability of peer funds, however, alternative assessments of performance may need to be considered.

3) Fees and Expenses

What the investment adviser charges for its services to each fund also is a focal point of the board's 15(c) evaluation. It is common for a board to compare the advisory fees charged to each fund with the fees charged by the adviser to other clients. This data normally is provided by the adviser. The Court in *Jones*, however, warned boards about potentially "inapt comparisons." According to the Court, "there may be significant differences between the services provided by an investment adviser to a mutual fund and those it provides to a pension fund. . . . If the services rendered are sufficiently different that a comparison is not probative, then courts must reject such a comparison. Even if the services provided and the fees charged to an independent fund are relevant, courts should be mindful that the Act does not necessarily ensure fee parity between mutual funds and institutional clients contrary to petitioners' [plaintiffs'] contentions."

Boards also typically consider fees charged by other investment advisers to funds with investments objectives and policies that are similar to the fund in question. This information normally is provided by, or based on information provided by, a third-party data provider. The Supreme Court also expressed reservations about these types of comparisons, warning against placing too much emphasis on a comparison of one fund's advisory fees against fees charged to other mutual funds by other advisers. "These comparisons are problematic because these fees . . . may not be the product of negotiations conducted at arm's length."

The Supreme Court's statements regarding fees should not be interpreted to mean that a review of fees is not important. Rather, those statements are a useful admonition to boards about focusing too narrowly on a single point of comparison or only one of the Gartenberg factors.

4) Profitability

The profitability of a particular advisory contract is one of the most difficult factors to analyze because, among other things, it generally requires an equitable allocation of the adviser's overall costs and expenses among the various funds and any other clients for whom it provides services. Courts have closely scrutinized costs and profitability data and methodologies. In so doing, the courts have acknowledged that there are many acceptable ways to allocate common costs, each of which could lead to a significantly different result. In general, a court should not invalidate a cost allocation methodology reviewed by independent directors if the methodology has a reasonable basis. Information about distribution costs is relevant to overall assessment of business arrangements, but it is important to identify and distinguish the marketing and promotional costs incurred by the adviser and its affiliates. If the adviser prepares the profitability information (as is usually the case), the information should be in a manner consistent with the information used by the adviser for internal management purposes or the adviser should explain the basis for any differences. Retaining an independent expert to assist in preparing a profitability study may prove helpful, especially to the extent the expert establishes or reviews the profitability methodology. An advisory fee does not violate Section 36(b) because it is highly profitable to the manager. Courts have consistently declined to set a limit on the profits an adviser can earn; one case where the fees were determined to meet the standard of Section 36(b) involved pre-tax margins of 59.1%, 66.8%, and 77.3% (for the periods 1979 through 1981), although the court acknowledged that it could have reached a different result under other circumstances.

5) Economies of Scale

With respect to economies of scale, the courts have concluded that the basic test is whether the directors can satisfy themselves that the information that is available provides a reasonable basis for judgment that the benefits of any economies of scale are equitably shared by the adviser with the fund (e.g., through contractual "break-points"; through fee or expense caps; by means of a fee structure that in effect incorporates economies of scale by virtue of a relatively low starting point which subsumes economies of scale throughout; or through reinvestment of profits to enhance services). It can be a challenge for an investment adviser and a board to know with certainty whether economies of scale exist vis-à-vis a particular fund and even more difficult (if not impossible) to ascertain the nature of those economies of scale and the asset size(s) at which they may exist. Thus, the information that boards consider in this regard often is based on a number of assumptions, detailed by the adviser and discussed with the board.

6) "Fall-out" Benefits

A "fall-out" benefit is essentially any benefit that the adviser or its affiliates derive from their relationship with the fund. These can include research procured by the adviser through brokerage commissions paid for by the fund, reputational benefits resulting from strong fund performance, the ability to more easily procure business from third parties as a result of the experience gained from providing services to the fund and other, similar benefits. The list of fall-out benefits can be quite broad. It is important to remember that fall-out benefits likely exist in every business relationship and their existence is neither wrong nor illegal. Directors must simply remember to consider them as they evaluate the investment advisory agreement and all the benefits that the adviser and its affiliates derive each year from that contract.

C. Disclosure Requirements as to Director Deliberations

Funds must provide detailed disclosure in shareholder reports and in certain proxy statements describing how their boards evaluate and approve their investment advisory arrangements. The disclosures must be reasonably detailed. According to the SEC, these disclosures aim to "ensure fair and reasonable" fund fees through increased transparency, which will encourage fund boards "to engage in vigorous and independent oversight of advisory contracts."

The fund's disclosure is required to include factors relating to both the board's selection of the investment adviser, and its approval of the advisory fee and any other amounts to be paid under the advisory contract. The fund is required to include a discussion as to specific factors, and how the board evaluated each factor, including, but not limited to, the following:

- the nature, extent, and quality of the services to be provided by the investment adviser;
- the investment performance of the fund and the investment adviser;
- the costs of the services to be provided and the profits to be realized by the investment adviser and its affiliates from the relationship with the fund;
- the extent to which economies of scale would be realized as the fund grows; and
- whether fee levels reflect these economies of scale for the benefit of fund investors.

The fund's discussion must indicate whether the board relied upon comparisons of the services to be rendered and the amounts to be paid under the advisory contract with those under other investment advisory contracts, such as contracts of the same and other investment advisers with other registered investment companies or of other types of clients (e.g., pension funds and other institutional investors). If the board relied upon such comparisons, the discussion would be required to describe the comparisons that were relied on and how they assisted the board in concluding that the contract should be approved.

As part of its examination program, the SEC staff reviews the 15(c) process in which boards approve advisory arrangements. Areas of review include whether the board devoted adequate time to its deliberations, information the board considered during its decision-making, and how the board applied the information considered. The SEC staff has indicated that it expects board meeting minutes to provide information regarding what the directors considered and that if the information does not contain sufficient detail, the SEC examiners may want to discuss the matter with the independent directors.

In 2013, in a case involving Northern Lights Compliance Services, LLC, the SEC settled administrative proceedings against the directors, including the independent directors, of two registered investment companies with multiple series funds, and the providers of administrative and chief compliance officer services to certain of the funds, based on disclosure, reporting, recordkeeping and compliance violations, including violations relating to disclosures regarding the directors' 15(c) evaluation process that the SEC considered "materially untrue or misleading." Among other things, the SEC found that: (1) certain disclosures stated that the board had received and considered comparisons of advisory fees charged by comparable mutual funds, whereas, in fact, such peer group data was not provided to or considered by the board; (2) certain disclosures stated that the board concluded that a fund's overall expenses were compared to a peer group of similarly managed funds and that the board concluded that the fund's advisory fees and expense ratio were acceptable in light of the quality of services provided and the level of fees paid by a peer group of similarly managed mutual funds. The SEC concluded that these statements "were materially misleading since they implied that the fund was paying fees that were not materially higher than the middle of its peer group range when, in fact, the adviser's approved fee was materially higher than all of the fees of the adviser's selected peer group of funds and nearly double the peer group's mean fees." The case highlights the need for a careful vetting of the information provided to boards during the 15(c) process and for directors to understand the process for ensuring the accuracy of the board meeting minutes and disclosures in shareholder reports relating to the factors considered and conclusions reached by the board when approving or renewing investment advisory contracts.

D. Sub-advisory Contracts and the Multi-manager Structure

Some advisers delegate responsibility for providing investment advisory and certain other services to one or more sub-advisers. Under the 1940 Act, sub-advisory contracts are regulated in the same manner as advisory contracts. This means that they must meet the Section 15 requirements described above (including requisite shareholder approval when necessary). A number of funds have been formed with, or subsequently have implemented, a manager-of-managers structure. Under this structure, the primary adviser typically maintains overall responsibility for the management of the fund (as well as certain administrative responsibilities) but hires one or more sub-advisers to manage some or all of the assets of the fund. The SEC has granted exemptive relief to certain funds that permits those funds, subject to a variety of conditions to hire new sub-advisers without obtaining shareholder approval for the new sub-advisory contract. Board approval is still required under such exemptive relief.

Sub-adviser arrangements come in different forms and the directors should have an understanding of the structure of the arrangements, including the services to be provided by the respective parties and the extent to which the primary adviser is responsible for providing oversight and monitoring of the sub-adviser. The directors should have an understanding as to how the fees and expenses associated with providing the services are allocated among the parties and determine their desired approach to providing oversight and monitoring of the sub-adviser.

In the current wave of Section 36(b) litigation, shareholders have challenged the advisory fee when there are both advisers and sub-advisers. The allegations include variations on a number of theories including: (1) that the adviser delegates all of the investment services to the sub-adviser, but nonetheless retains a large fee for little or no services; or (2) the adviser charges its fund clients more for investment advisory services than it charges unaffiliated funds for which it serves as sub-adviser. A description of the services that the adviser and sub-adviser provide to the fund is an important part of explaining the reasons that the board approved the challenged fee. Similarly, providing information to fund boards about the fees that the adviser charges as sub-adviser to similar funds assists the board in reviewing the nature and quality of service, as well as comparable fees for those services.

Boards sometimes find that reviewing profitability in the sub-advisory context can be difficult because sub-advisers may be unwilling to share profitability information or their expense allocations with third parties. As a result, some boards place less emphasis on a sub-adviser's profitability but instead rely on the notion that the sub-advisory fee has been negotiated at arms' length with the adviser.

E. Other Arrangements with Affiliates

When a fund engages the adviser or its affiliates to perform services such as transfer agency, custodial, valuation, or bookkeeping services, special consideration by the fund board is required. These other service arrangements are generally permissible. Based upon positions taken by the SEC staff, the independent directors should determine that (i) the service contract is in the best interests of the fund and its shareholders, (ii) the services are required for the operation of the fund, (iii) the services are of a nature and quality at least equal to the same or similar services provided by independent third parties, and (iv) the fees for those services are fair and reasonable in light of the usual and customary fees charged by service providers for services of the same nature and quality. Payments to the adviser or its affiliates for other services may be subject to the fiduciary standards of Section 36(b).

F. Change of Control of the Investment Adviser or Distributor; Assignment

In the event of a change of control of the adviser or distributor, or any transaction that operates as an assignment of contracts, the fund's investment advisory or distribution agreement is terminated by operation of law. In these events, the 1940 Act requires that the board of directors consider the approval of new investment advisory and distribution arrangements, considering the relevant factors discussed in this Section 5 for advisers and in Section 6 for distributors. Any new management arrangement must then be approved by shareholders. In considering the proposal of the existing adviser or distributor to continue under new agreements, emphasis should be placed upon any changes in the surviving entity's plans generally with respect to the fund, including the manner in which the portfolio management, administrative, distribution, and other services will be provided and the extent to which new personnel, methods, and systems will be used.

Many corporate transactions, including the sale of an adviser or a parent of the adviser, are deemed to be a change of control, which triggers this provision. Typically, the parties to the transaction seek to obtain shareholder approval of a new advisory agreement before the transaction actually takes place. Sometimes, however, the nature of the transaction makes it difficult to secure shareholder approval of a new advisory agreement in advance of the transaction. In these types of circumstances, an adviser can continue to provide advisory services to a fund after a change of control under an interim contract for up to 150 days, subject to certain conditions and determinations by the directors.

A change of control of an investment adviser often implicates Section 15(f) of the 1940 Act. This section provides a safe harbor for an adviser that sells or assigns its fund advisory business for profit, provided the transaction satisfies two requirements: (i) for three years thereafter, at least 75% of the fund's board of directors must not be interested persons of either the adviser or the predecessor adviser, and (ii) for two years, no "unfair burden" (such as an increase in advisory or distribution costs) may be imposed upon the fund as a result of the transaction. Most acquisitions of advisers are structured to comply with the terms of Section 15(f). The predecessor adviser and the successor adviser each may represent and warrant that the transaction will not impose an unfair burden upon the funds. In addition, typically, the predecessor adviser and/or the successor adviser undertakes to pay all the fund's costs associated with approving the new advisory agreement. In the absence of compliance with Section 15(f), an investment adviser could face legal challenges to its right to retain profits on the sale of its business.

Board Responsibilities with Respect to Distribution Arrangements

A. Importance of an Effective Distribution System

Mutual funds typically continuously offer their shares and are obligated to redeem their shares at the next determined net asset value within seven days of receipt of the redemption order. A fund's ability to suspend the right of redemption is very limited. For this reason, the creation and maintenance of an effective distribution system for a mutual fund's shares is an essential goal of any mutual fund sponsor. Such a system is essential to build and maintain an asset base adequate for portfolio management, to offset decreases in fund assets attributable to redemptions, and to permit realization of economies of scale. Distribution activities are typically conducted through a general or limited-purpose broker-dealer (referred to as the "distributor") that is registered with the SEC as a broker-dealer and that is a member of FINRA. The distributor serves as a fund's principal underwriter and typically oversees the marketing of the fund's shares. The distributor is often an affiliate of the fund's sponsor. The distributor may sell shares directly and/or through unaffiliated dealers or financial service intermediaries that enter into selling agreements with the distributor. "Load" funds typically impose a sales charge upon the sale of fund shares; "no-load" funds sell their shares at net asset value without any sales charge (although no-load fund supermarkets may charge their own transaction fees). The distribution costs of no-load funds can be paid by Rule 12b-1 fees (discussed below). The advisers or sponsors of both load and no-load funds can, and frequently do, finance fund distribution with payments out of the adviser's or sponsor's own revenues or assets.

B. Distribution Financing Techniques

In 1980, the SEC adopted Rule 12b-1 which permits funds, subject to largely procedural conditions, to directly incur marketing and promotional expenses. The rule prohibits an open-end fund from using its own assets to pay for any marketing or promotional expenses unless it has adopted a Rule 12b-1 plan and the payments are made pursuant to the plan. Utilizing Rule 12b-1, the fund industry has developed a wide variety of methods for compensating broker-dealers and others that sell or otherwise assist in the distribution of fund shares. These include front-end and contingent deferred sales charges and ongoing asset-based distribution fees. Many funds that do not charge front-end sales loads have established Rule 12b-1 plans to pay relatively low amounts (sometimes referred to as "service fees") to compensate sales personnel and others for providing ongoing services to shareholders. Under FINRA rules, service fee rates may not exceed 0.25% of net assets and funds paying 12b-1 and service fees aggregating greater than 0.25% may not refer to themselves as "no-load" funds. FINRA has clarified that for purposes of the 0.25% limit on "service fees," the limit only applies to shareholder liaison services or customer service fees, and does not apply to fees for other services, such as sub-transfer agency, sub-accounting, or record-keeping services.

Funds are permitted to issue multiple classes of shares representing interests in the same portfolio of securities, but with each class subject to a different distribution arrangement. An alternative to the single (or one-tier) fund with multiple classes is a master-feeder structure in which one or more funds (the "feeder funds") invest all of their assets in another fund (the "master fund"). All portfolio management services are performed, and related costs borne, at the master fund level, with distribution and shareholder services performed, and related costs borne, at the feeder fund level. It is possible to combine the two structures by having feeder funds issue multiple classes of shares.

Many funds offer investors alternative sales charge arrangements combining, through multi-class and/or master-feeder structures, front-end and deferred sales charge methods. They also utilize different combinations of service fees, distribution fees, and conversion features from one class to a lower-fee rate class once a specified maximum payment level or a specified time period has been achieved.

Investors can also buy and redeem shares of many funds through "fund supermarket" or retirement plan platforms sponsored by third-party intermediaries, such as broker-dealers, retirement plan administrators, and other institutions. The sponsors of these platforms offer their customers access to large numbers of funds from numerous fund complexes, and provide sub-transfer agency, sub-administration, and/or distribution services to the funds whose shares are made available on the platforms. (See Section 6.D(8) for a discussion of payments to third-party intermediaries.)

C. Revenue Sharing and Shelf Space Payments

For many years, broker-dealers and other financial intermediaries have increasingly sought compensation from fund advisers and distributors for distribution in addition to the compensation received from the funds and fund investors in sales loads and Rule 12b-1 fees. Such payments, which are made from the adviser's or distributor's own resources, are generally referred to as "revenue sharing" payments. Revenue sharing payments can cover a wide range of distribution or administrative services and revenue sharing payment arrangements vary. They may include annual payments by a fund sponsor to an intermediary based on: average net assets of a fund attributable to customers of the intermediary; gross sales to customers of the intermediary; and the intermediary making the fund's shares available for sale to its clients of the intermediary or including them on "preferred lists." These last types of revenue sharing payments are often referred to as payments for "shelf space." Revenue sharing had also been made through the allocation of fund brokerage to reward sales (referred to as directed brokerage arrangements), but this practice was banned by amendments to Rule 12b-1 in 2004 (see Section 6.D(5)).

Revenue sharing arrangements (including shelf space payments) have been a well-established practice for a number of years and have been well known to the SEC, FINRA, and other regulators. Revenue sharing can raise a number of legal issues, specifically, whether the payments should be made pursuant to Rule 12b-1 plans and whether revenue sharing practices create potential conflicts of interest that require disclosure by the fund and/or the broker-dealer or platform provider. One concern about revenue sharing arrangements is that they may create a monetary incentive for an intermediary to recommend one fund over another that may conflict with the interests of the investor. The same incentive exists when intermediaries receive extra compensation for selling certain fund shares or fund share classes (referred to as differential compensation).

The principal Rule 12b-1 issue with revenue sharing is whether the payments are made out of legitimate (i.e., not excessive) profits from the adviser's contract with the fund (or otherwise out of its own resources) or whether they constitute an indirect use of the fund's assets to finance the distribution of its shares and therefore must be made pursuant to a duly adopted Rule 12b-1 plan. The SEC has stated that fund directors, particularly the independent directors, are primarily responsible for determining whether revenue-sharing payments constitute an indirect use of a fund's assets for distribution. If the board has concluded that the fees paid to the adviser or its affiliates are appropriate compensation for the services provided, then it can conclude that the source of any revenue sharing payments made by the adviser is the adviser's legitimate profits and that, therefore, the payments are not required to be made pursuant to a Rule 12b-1 plan.

The SEC, FINRA, and certain states have brought a number of enforcement actions against fund groups and broker-dealers for failure to make appropriate disclosure to investors of conflicts of interest arising from shelf space payments. For a number of years, many funds have made disclosures in their prospectuses or Statements of Additional Information about their adviser's or distributor's revenue-sharing payments to broker-dealers. The nature of the disclosures has varied considerably, with much of the disclosure being quite general. In response to the enforcement actions, some fund groups have expanded their disclosures of revenue sharing arrangements. The expanded disclosures include such information as a description of the shelf space services being paid for, the amounts paid for such services, the broker-dealers' *quid pro quo* obligations under the arrangements, and disclosures as to the conflicts of interest resulting from the revenue sharing arrangements. In 2004, the SEC proposed new disclosure requirements to require broker-dealers to provide their customers specified information regarding distribution costs and conflicts of interest at both the point of sale and in confirmations, but the proposal was never adopted.

D. Board Responsibilities

1) Regulation of Distribution Arrangements

Like an investment advisory agreement, a distribution agreement between a fund and its distributor must be re-evaluated and re-approved annually by a majority of the fund's directors, including a majority of the fund's independent directors. No shareholder approval is required for a distribution agreement. As noted above, a distribution agreement may not provide for the expenditure of fund assets that is primarily intended to result in the sale of fund shares unless such expenditure is covered by a duly-adopted Rule 12b-1 plan.

Separately, advertising and sales literature are regulated by both the SEC and FINRA. FINRA's Conduct Rules regulate all types of sales-related charges, imposing regulatory maximums on both front-end and ongoing asset-based charges.

2) General Responsibilities for Distribution

Little guidance is found in the 1940 Act or in SEC rules or interpretive materials concerning the factors that should be considered by a board of directors in approving distribution arrangements and fees. Directors should understand the proposed plan of distribution—to whom and by whom shares are expected to be sold—and the distribution costs to be incurred. The board should monitor the performance of the distributor and receive regular reports on the sales and redemptions of fund shares and the revenues and costs of the selling function, as well as the proper application of sales load limits and breakpoints. Lawsuits filed several years ago have sought to question the legality of retaining a Rule 12b-1 plan (or at least continuing to assess Rule 12b-1 fees) on a mutual fund that has been closed to new investors. The lawsuits claim, among other things, that a mutual fund closed to new investors or to taking additional assets has no need for distribution services. Targeted mutual funds and other defendants in those cases have asserted defenses (such as the need to pay for past services, to continue to pay for services to existing shareholders in order not to lose fund assets or to repay financiers of distribution activities), and the courts generally have agreed.

3) Oversight of Rule 12b-1 Plans

As noted above, a Rule 12b-1 plan is the exclusive means by which an open-end fund may use its assets to bear the cost of distributing its shares. Before a fund's assets can be used for distribution purposes, a Rule 12b-1 plan (and agreements relating to the plan) must be approved by the fund's directors and, if adopted after the issuance of shares of the class, by the shareholders of that class of fund shares. The procedural requirements of Rule 12b-1 specify that the approval must be made by the board as a whole and separately by the independent directors who have no direct or indirect financial interest in the operation of the plan or in any agreements related to the plan. Rule 12b-1 is among those exemptive rules that are available only to funds that satisfy the SEC Governance Standards.

Once adopted, the continuance of the plan and each related agreement must be approved on an annual basis by the board in the same manner as the initial approval and must be terminable without penalty at any time by the independent directors or terminable by a vote of the fund's shareholders without penalty upon not more than 60 days' written notice to the affected parties. A Rule 12b-1 plan may not be amended to materially increase the amounts payable under the plan without approval by the fund's shareholders. The board must review payments made under the Rule 12b-1 plan on a quarterly basis.

To approve a Rule 12b-1 plan, the board must conclude that the plan is reasonably likely to benefit the fund and its shareholders. The rule provides that in considering whether a fund should implement or continue a Rule 12b-1 plan the directors of the fund shall have a duty to request and evaluate, and any person who is a party to any agreement with the fund relating to the plan shall have a duty to furnish, such information as shall be reasonably necessary to an informed determination of whether such plan should be implemented or continued. It further provides that the directors should consider and give appropriate weight to all pertinent factors, and that minutes describing the factors considered and the basis for the decision to use fund assets for distribution must be made and preserved. A fundamental factor to be considered in connection with Rule 12b-1 plans is whether the distribution method under consideration provides for a reasonable financing alternative under the facts and circumstances of the particular fund and the type of investor to which the plan is directed. If a distributor is the fund's adviser or affiliated with the fund's adviser, Rule 12b-1 distribution payments to that distributor may be subject to the fiduciary standards of Section 36(b) of the 1940 Act.

When Rule 12b-1 was adopted in 1980, the SEC suggested a non-exclusive series of factors that directors should consider when evaluating a 12b-1 plan and determining whether there is a reasonable likelihood that continuation of the plan will benefit the fund and its shareholders. While directors and others have observed that the factors outlined by the SEC in 1980 appear somewhat outdated and the SEC staff has acknowledged as much, the factors have not been updated by the SEC. Nonetheless, directors continue to review the factors when considering the approval or renewal of a 12b-1 plan, typically acknowledging that some may be more relevant than others. The factors are as follows: (1) the nature of the problem or circumstances which make implementation of the plan necessary or appropriate; (2) the causes of such problems or circumstances; (3) the way in which the plan would address these problems or circumstances and how it would be expected to resolve or alleviate them, including the nature and approximate amount of the expenditures, the relationship of the expenditures to the overall cost structure of the fund, the nature of the anticipated benefits, and the time it would take for those benefits to be achieved; (4) the merits of possible alternative plans; (5) the interrelationship between the plan and the activities of any other person who might finance or has financed the distribution of the fund's shares, including whether any payments by the fund to such other person are made in such a manner as to constitute the indirect financing by the fund for distribution; (6) the possible benefits of the plan to any other person relative to those expected to inure to the fund; (7) whether the plan has in fact produced the benefits anticipated for the fund and its shareholders; and (8) the need for independent counsel or experts to assist the trustees in reaching a determination.

Directors also may consider the factors outlined in the MFDF's "Best Practices and Practical Guidance for Directors under Rule 12b-1" issued in 2007, which includes the following factors, among others: (1) how a fund's 12b-1 plan fits into the fund's overall distribution plan;

(2) whether continued distribution through the fund's existing interme-
diate channels is in the best interests of the fund's shareholders; (3) how
continued distribution of fund shares, and, in particular, the use of fund
assets to pay for distribution, will potentially benefit fund shareholders;
(4) whether there is a need of the fund to penetrate particular distribution channels in the marketplace, as well as the competitive conditions
within those channels; (5) whether fund shareholders (or shareholders
of a particular class) have effectively agreed to pay specific amounts to
support distribution of the fund to them; (6) whether the cost of the
service being furnished through a 12b-1 plan is reasonable in light of
the nature of the service generally and the quality of the specific service
being obtained; and (7) when a fund is closed to new investors, whether
there is a need to repay amounts already spent distributing the fund that
warrants continuance of the plan.

In 2010, the SEC proposed to rescind Rule 12b-1 and proposed a
new rule, Rule 12b-2, which would restructure the regulatory framework for payments by mutual funds for the marketing and distribution
of fund shares. The proposal would continue to allow the use of fund
assets to pay for distribution expenses, but would implement a new
approach to regulating such payments. This new approach would break
out the types of fees currently paid pursuant to Rule 12b-1 into two
components—ongoing fees for marketing and services (subject to a fee
cap of 25 basis points per year), and ongoing asset-based sales charges
that would be in excess of the marketing and service fee as an alternative
to a traditional front-end sales load, subject to a cumulative fee cap on
sales charges. Although the proposal was unanimously approved by the
SEC for public comment, it has not been adopted or re-proposed and is
not believed to be an SEC priority.

4) Review of Multiple Class Arrangements

The use of multiple share classes is integral to many fund distribution
plans, permitting shareholders to purchase shares under different load
arrangements, and permitting funds to pay for access to different intermediary distribution channels or different services. Before a fund issues
multiple classes of shares, a majority of the directors, and a majority of the
independent directors, must approve a written plan required by Rule 18f-3
under the 1940 Act setting forth the separate shareholder service and/or

distribution arrangements for each class, the expense allocation for each class and any related conversion features or exchange privileges. The directors must find that the plan is in the best interests of each class and the fund as a whole. In making this finding, the board must focus on, among other things, the relationship among the classes and examine potential conflicts of interest among classes regarding allocation of fees, services and voting rights. The board must also consider the level of services provided to each class and the cost of those services to ensure that the services are appropriate and that the allocation of expenses is reasonable.

5) Prohibition on Directing Portfolio Transactions to Promote Sales of Fund Shares

In 2004, Rule 12b-1 was amended to prohibit the directing of a Fund's portfolio transactions to finance distribution. The amendments prohibit funds from compensating a broker-dealer for promoting or selling fund shares by directing portfolio transactions to that broker-dealer; including through "step-out" arrangements (where a broker-dealer executing a trade may "step out" a portion of the commission to pay the broker-dealer who distributes the fund's shares) and similar arrangements designed to compensate broker-dealers for selling fund shares. The amendments require any fund (or its adviser) that directs portfolio securities transactions to a broker-dealer selling the fund's shares to implement policies and procedures reasonably designed to ensure that its selection of broker-dealers to effect transactions is not influenced by considerations regarding the sale of fund shares. The fund's board of directors, including a majority of its independent directors, must approve the policies and procedures.

6) Consideration of Imposition of a Short-term Redemption Fee

Under Rule 22c-2, an open-end fund's board of directors, including a majority of the independent directors, must make a determination to either impose a redemption fee not to exceed 2% on shares redeemed within seven days of purchase or determine that a redemption fee is not necessary or appropriate. The rule is intended to address potential dilution associated with market timing and does not apply to money market funds, exchange traded funds, and funds that expressly permit market timing.

7) Monitoring of Sales Practices

A fund generally does not have direct legal responsibility for the activities of its distributor, selling broker-dealers, or other financial intermediaries involved in the distribution of the fund's shares including sales literature and advertisements. The fund is also not required to determine the suitability of its shares for the customers of selling broker-dealers. The activities of broker-dealers are regulated by the SEC and FINRA. The dealer agreements that distributors have with selling dealers typically provide that dealers must comply with the applicable rules and regulations regarding the sale of fund shares, including providing the benefit of the established breakpoints in share transactions.

Alleged improper sales practices have resulted in litigation and enforcement proceedings against brokers selling the funds. In such matters, the fund and its management were often not responsible for the violations and were not involved in the proceedings. The SEC has addressed the role of directors and their responsibilities with respect to such problems at the broker-dealer or intermediary level in connection with late trading and market timing allegations, as well as problems in the calculation of front-end sales load breakpoints and suitability issues in the sale of Class B shares. In the case of the late trading and market timing allegations, the SEC requested fund groups to promptly seek assurances from their selling broker-dealers and other intermediaries that they are following all relevant rules and regulations as well as internal policies and procedures, regarding the handling of mutual fund orders on a timely basis. The directors should monitor efforts of this kind.

As part of its compliance program (see Section 9), the fund distributor should monitor and oversee sales and marketing practices. The directors should monitor the distributor's efforts in this regard as part of their general oversight responsibilities, and focus on whether the distributor's compliance procedures are reasonably designed with respect to oversight of the activities of selling broker-dealers and intermediaries, including intermediaries holding shares in omnibus accounts (see Section 6.D(8)).

8) Payments to Third-party Intermediaries for Distribution and/or Sub-transfer Agency Services

Many investors in mutual funds buy and sell their shares through intermediaries, such as broker-dealers, retirement plan administrators and other institutions. In some cases these arrangements are referred to as "supermarkets" as a broker-dealer may make a very large number of funds available to investors that access its "platform." A common structure for these arrangements is aggregated accounts, often referred to as "omnibus" accounts. In this type of arrangement, an intermediary has one or more accounts with a mutual fund and the intermediary maintains the underlying shareholder account information and manages all interactions with and servicing of the underlying shareholders. As a result, the underlying shareholders in an omnibus account rarely interact directly with a mutual fund complex, and the fund complex may have little, if any, knowledge about such underlying shareholders. In a typical arrangement, the intermediary provides sub-transfer agency or other non-distribution services to the funds and their shareholders. (These services may include shareholder servicing or administrative services.) The intermediary may also contract to provide distribution services on behalf of the funds' principal underwriter. In return, the intermediary typically receives a fee for the services that it provides. This fee may be paid by the fund and/or the fund's investment adviser or distributor (such a payment by the adviser or distributor is often referred to as a "revenue sharing" payment). (See Section 6.C for a discussion of the directors' responsibility for determining whether revenue-sharing payments from fund assets constitute an indirect use of fund assets for distribution and therefore must be made pursuant to a Rule 12b-1 plan.)

As discussed in Section 6.B, Rule 12b-1 prohibits an open-end fund from using its own assets to pay for any distribution expenses (i.e., marketing or promotional expenses) outside of a Rule 12b-1 plan. The SEC staff's views on the issues arising under Rule 12b-1 from a fund's participation in platforms sponsored by third-party intermediaries and the board's role in reviewing payments to those intermediaries are outlined in an interpretive letter the SEC staff issued to the ICI in 1998 (the "Fund Supermarket Letter"). (The Fund Supermarket Letter is not a statement by the SEC, nor is it an SEC rule, but it is nonetheless the only written regulatory guidance on the subject issued to date.)

The Fund Supermarket Letter essentially sets forth a two-prong test. First, are some or all of the payments for services primarily intended to result in the sale of fund shares that may be deemed distribution services? If so, then, second, does the fund make some or all of the payments outside of a Rule 12b-1 plan? If the answer to both of these questions is yes, then the fund board must take certain steps to determine whether fund assets are being used to pay for distribution services outside of a Rule 12b-1 plan. (Some funds adopt so-called 'defensive' Rule 12b-1 plans to cover both the distribution and administrative services provided by an intermediary.)

The determination of whether any portion of a fee paid by a fund is primarily for distribution is a question of fact to be made by the fund's board and necessarily entails considering the nature of the services provided to the fund by the intermediary. Factors a board may consider include: the intermediary's characterization of the services that it offers; the specific services for which the fund or its distributor have contracted with the intermediary; the distributor's good-faith characterization of those services; whether the services provide any distribution benefits; whether the services provide non-distribution-related benefits and are typically provided by fund service providers; whether pension plan administrators and others with minimal distribution capability charge a similar fee for their administrative, recordkeeping and shareholder services; and whether an intermediary charges a lower fee if a fund closes to new investors, so that no distribution is taking place for a period of time.

The SEC staff clarified in the Fund Supermarket Letter that, if a fund pays all of the intermediary's fees from its Rule 12b-1 plan, then the fund board need not determine whether any portion of the fees are for non-distribution-related activities. Further, a fund board may determine that no portion of the fee paid from fund assets to an intermediary is for distribution services, for example if shares of a fund or class are no longer sold by the intermediary and that intermediary continues to provide services to existing shareholders of that fund or class.

If the board determines that some or all of the payments to an intermediary *are* for non-distribution services, then the board should determine whether the payments are reasonable in relation to: (1) the value of the non-distribution services provided by the intermediary and the benefits received by the fund and its shareholders; and (2) the payments that the fund would be required to make to another entity to perform the same services. There are many practical challenges to this determination, including that many fund groups have hundreds of intermediary arrangements; intermediaries are often compensated in different ways (based on assets or number of accounts); services vary by intermediary; intermediaries tend to limit the amount of information on their services that they will share with funds; and intermediaries may be chosen based on their distribution capabilities or profile rather than their shareholder servicing capabilities. In reviewing the reasonableness of the fees paid to an intermediary for sub-transfer agency and other non-distribution services, boards may review how those fees compare to the fees paid to the fund's transfer agent or other intermediaries (and how the services compare). They also may consider the basis on which intermediaries are compensated and why; and the general nature of the services provided by the intermediaries.

The increased use of third-party intermediaries to sell funds and/ or service their shareholders, and a corresponding increase in the fees charged by some intermediaries to provide these services, prompted the SEC staff to conduct national sweep examinations in 2013 and 2014, which it called 'payments for distribution in guise.' This title is intended to highlight whether a payment to an intermediary from fund assets is a legitimate payment for sub-transfer agency or other non-distribution services or in reality a portion of such payment is for shelf space so the intermediary will include the fund as an investment option on its platform and sell the fund's shares. Areas of focus in these exams included the adequacy of disclosures made to fund boards about payments to third-party intermediaries and the boards' oversight of those payments. The SEC staff has indicated that it may consider issuing guidance in this area or it may recommend that the SEC propose new regulations following the completion and review of the information obtained during these sweep exams. The SEC staff has also indicated that enforcement proceedings are expected to be brought as a result of certain finding made during the sweep examinations.

Directors should also consider how the fund sponsor and the fund's chief compliance officer oversee the intermediaries' compliance with fund policies (such as those relating to redemption fees, reductions, or waivers of sales charges, and frequent trading) and applicable laws and regulations (such as privacy and anti-money laundering). Many fund groups have enhanced their due diligence review of compliance by intermediaries with these fund policies. The fund complexes seek information from the intermediaries, either through certifications or questionnaires developed by the funds or internal control reports provided by the intermediaries, regarding the intermediaries' operational capabilities and regulatory compliance (see Section 9).

Statutory, Regulatory, and Oversight Responsibilities

A. Oversight Responsibilities

1) General Responsibilities

Investment company operations are subject to many requirements flowing from statutes, rules and regulations, court and regulatory decisions, and rules of self-regulatory organizations. Funds also have investment policies and limitations, including fundamental policies and limitations that only shareholders can vote to change. Funds must comply with policies and limitations found in fund prospectuses; charters and by-laws; board-adopted resolutions; and conditions contained in SEC exemptive orders and no-action or interpretative letters. To qualify for the "pass-through" tax treatment afforded "regulated investment companies" under Subchapter M of the Internal Revenue Code, funds must also comply with a number of highly technical tax requirements.

In 2013, the staff of the SEC released guidance reminding funds and advisers of their obligations to comply with representations and conditions contained in SEC exemptive orders. The guidance suggested that firms adopt and implement policies and procedures reasonably designed to ensure ongoing compliance with representations and conditions contained in such orders—and the related applications—for exemptive relief. The same principles apply to representations and conditions contained in no-action or interpretative letters. The staff suggested that the adequacy and effectiveness of all such policies and procedures be reviewed on an annual basis.

Fund directors are responsible for oversight and do not manage funds on a day-to-day basis. As a practical matter, the directors cannot ensure that funds comply with all their compliance policies and procedures. The board typically oversees the execution of these responsibilities by the fund's investment adviser, administrator, custodian, and other service providers who are responsible for the ongoing operations of the fund.

Although the independent directors are expected to act as "watch-dogs" for the shareholders, they are not expected to discover compliance failures on their own initiative. Instead, they may satisfy their responsibility by adopting and monitoring the fund's compliance program and meeting regularly with the fund's CCO (see Section 9). The compliance responsibilities of directors are heightened when conflicts of interest or special problems exist.

The directors should carefully monitor the overall business operations of investment companies. This process has been described as one of "kicking the tires, looking for warning flags." This is usually done through a series of written and oral reports provided by service providers and the CCO periodically throughout the year, often in connection with regular and special board meetings. The directors may request reports to address matters requiring their review or approval under SEC rules or that they believe are necessary to satisfy their general oversight duties. Directors should monitor these operations with a view toward assessing the quality of the risk management procedures and internal controls and monitoring the effectiveness of compliance procedures (see Section 7.A(3)). Frequently, monitoring involves considering issues that reflect on the quality of the fund management services or the quality of other service providers' compliance with applicable rules and regulations. In considering the adequacy of compliance controls and procedures, directors should seek assurance from the fund management that they are monitoring the other service providers and intermediaries as part of their compliance program.

See the Regulatory Calendar in Appendix A for a list of significant matters to which fund boards or their audit committees have specific responsibilities.

2) Monitoring Conflicts of Interest

The central role of independent directors in monitoring conflicts of interest between advisers and their funds has been evolving and increasing. The SEC encourages directors to be an "independent force in fund affairs" rather than passively accepting the recommendations of management. The SEC has urged fund directors to bring to the boardroom "a high degree of rigor and skeptical objectivity to the evaluation of management and its plans and proposals," particularly when evaluating conflicts of interest. Directors should be "highly skeptical" of arguments that merely rationalize the resolution of conflicts in favor of the fund adviser, the SEC has stated, and should seek results that advance the best interests of fund shareholders.

How can directors identify conflicts of interest? They can start by reviewing any arrangement involving the use of fund assets to pay for services. Some of these arrangements are obvious, such as the investment advisory agreement and other agreements with fund affiliates. Some are not so obvious. They may involve soft dollars to pay for research or other services, securities lending, and other arrangements in which funds pay for services directly or indirectly. Experience demonstrates that conflicts can arise in ways that are difficult to detect, such as the allocation of investment opportunities among the adviser's clients, market timing or late trading. While funds have taken steps to mitigate these particular conflicts of interest, directors should be vigilant to identify other areas that may give rise to conflicts. The MFDF best practices report recommends that boards establish a process for identifying and reviewing conflicts of interest and consider assigning to a committee of the board the express responsibility for addressing potential conflicts of interest that may arise between the fund and its adviser or affiliates due to other business activities of the adviser or affiliates.

3) Overseeing Risk Management, Internal Controls, and Compliance Procedures

It is important that investment advisers, as well as others to whom responsibilities have been delegated, maintain effective risk management, internal control, and compliance procedures. In its inspection process, the SEC staff focuses on the risk assessment process and the development of internal controls that form the basis for the compliance program. If in its analysis the SEC staff determines that the adviser has weak internal controls, it will be labeled as high risk and will be inspected accordingly.

There is no single correct way for boards to monitor risk management, internal control, and compliance procedures. Directors should have a basic understanding of how risks, especially risks involving conflicts, are identified on an ongoing basis, how appropriate controls are developed and implemented, and the extent to which forensic testing is used to monitor and audit the effectiveness of the procedures. An example of forensic testing is analyzing trading patterns to identify anomalous trades (such as unexpectedly profitable trades, concentration of trading with particular counterparties, and the like). Knowledgeable compliance and operational personnel, with established lines of authority, should be responsible for implementing compliance and risk management procedures. These personnel, who should understand the importance of effective compliance and control functions and the consequences of failures, should be accountable to senior management. A very important component of any control function is the support of senior management and its ability to foster a firm-wide commitment to the observance of sound practices (the so-called "tone at the top"). It is important that the internal controls be uniformly applied and that no personnel (i.e., "stars") or business lines are exempt from the rules. The SEC staff has stated that in its assessment of the compliance and risk management culture in an organization, it seeks to determine how seriously the organization takes compliance and risk management and considers staffing, funding, and other indicia of a properly resourced control function. In recent years, the SEC staff has expressed a willingness to communicate separately with the board, especially when it has substantial compliance concerns due to repeated violations or generally based on its perception of the tone at the top. Further, in certain instances, the SEC staff has sought to interview independent directors about a particular practice or decision. Independent directors should consult with counsel as to how best to respond to such requests.

Directors should understand the elements of effective compliance, risk management, and other controls, including training programs and written manuals, checklists, and procedures for portfolio managers, traders, marketers, valuation specialists, and other key personnel. Directors typically seek to learn about the structure of a firm's controls through reports from, or meetings with, the heads of the different control functions over time. Directors should inquire about the due diligence efforts management employs in its review of control functions maintained by third-party service providers. Directors also should discuss the adequacy of internal controls and compliance procedures with the fund's chief financial officer, CCO, independent auditors and internal auditors, if any. For most funds the internal auditors fund directors may meet with will be employees of the adviser with responsibility to the adviser's audit committee rather than that of the fund. Under the Sarbanes-Oxley Act's mandated certification process, the principal executive and financial officers of a fund must certify that they have disclosed to the auditors and the audit committee all significant deficiencies and material weaknesses in the design or operation of internal control over financial reporting and any fraud, whether material or not, that involves management or other employees who have a significant role in the fund's internal control over financial reporting.

Boards should confirm that advisers inform them when the SEC schedules an inspection relating to a fund in their complex and the results of any exit interview. They should also receive copies of any deficiency letter. The directors can then review with management the response to the deficiency letter and consider with management any issues that appear to require the board's attention. Similar procedures may be appropriate for FINRA inspections of the distributor's activities and the PCAOB's inspection of the audit firm as it relates to a fund audit.

In the wake of the financial crisis that commenced in 2008, regulators, investors, intermediaries, and other constituencies greatly increased their emphasis on risk management as a separate control function from, for example, compliance or internal audit programs. Risk management is understood as involving several steps. These include maintaining—and keeping current—an inventory of the firm's investment, operational, valuation, legal, compliance, and other risks and considering how each risk might be both quantified and, if appropriate, mitigated. With the increased attention paid to risk management, there also has been an increase in the number of firms that have a designated chief risk officer and the number of boards that have a designated body responsible for oversight of risk management. Finally, it is a requirement that boards of public companies generally, including investment companies, disclose in their public filings a description of the board's role in the oversight of risk management, whether the board has a designated risk committee, and the relationship between the board and senior management in respect of risk management.

B. Portfolio Management

1) Investment Oversight

Although fund directors are not expected to play an active role in managing a fund's investments, they are responsible for overseeing generally the fund's investment performance and monitoring investment practices.

Investment performance is obviously one of the factors considered by the directors when they consider renewing the advisory contract. Directors should also monitor fund investment performance during the year through regular performance reports from management with references to appropriate performance measurement indices and the performance of similar funds.

The directors should also require focused performance presentations on a regular basis, including special written reports and oral presentations by portfolio managers with an opportunity for discussion with the directors. In monitoring performance, the directors should consider the adequacy of the investment staffing and resources provided by the investment adviser in performing its duties. If a fund's performance deteriorates, the directors should consider what steps, if any, appear necessary to address the situation. Some fund groups address the directors' concerns in this regard by establishing "watch lists," which identify under-performing funds and describe specific corrective measures they are taking.

The investment adviser is responsible for managing the fund's portfolio in a manner that is consistent with the fund's investment objective, policies and restrictions. As part of their general oversight of investments, directors should be alert for any material deviations from these requirements. Directors should also use the investment performance oversight process to build their understanding of the risks inherent in the fund's investment strategies.

As part of oversight of a fund's investment operations and results, directors should oversee and monitor the fund's use of derivatives. The SEC staff has emphasized that directors play an important role in overseeing a fund's use of derivatives. Particular areas of emphasis that the regulators have singled out include:

- Prospectus and statement of additional information disclosure of policies and limitations regarding the use of derivatives,

- How funds value derivatives,
- Liquidity of the derivatives, and
- Adequate compliance programs, operational systems, risk management and internal controls, relating to derivatives.

The directors should consider whether the degree of fund use of derivatives make it appropriate to receive from management regular reports concerning fund use of derivatives. These presentations may include such information as the extent of the fund's use of derivatives, the specific purposes of strategies using derivatives, the success of those strategies, the resulting risk exposure, the effectiveness of internal controls designed to monitor risk, and the extent to which such activities have (and in the future may) affect performance. In their review of derivatives activities, the directors may rely upon knowledgeable individuals or experts, including those on the adviser's staff or outside experts. Generally, directors should seek to reach a comfort level with respect to the adviser's ability to utilize derivatives effectively and to manage any attendant risk. (See Section 10 for additional discussion on oversight of derivatives and alternative investment strategies.)

2) Portfolio Trading Practices

Fund directors must oversee adviser portfolio trading practices. Although directors are not expected to monitor a fund's individual trades, they are expected to monitor the adviser's general trading procedures and guidelines. Brokerage commissions are assets of the fund, and the fund's directors are responsible for understanding and reviewing policies governing brokerage practices. The directors should also monitor the adviser's practices with respect to portfolio transactions conducted on a principal basis in the dealer market. Fixed-income securities, including money market securities, as well as many types of derivatives, are generally traded on a principal basis.

As part of their general oversight obligations, independent directors are expected to monitor the process by which an adviser seeks "best execution" of trades made on behalf of the fund. In a 2003 concept release seeking comment on a number of issues related to the disclosure of mutual fund transaction costs, the SEC stated that although the investment adviser has an obligation to seek the best execution of securities transactions arranged for or on behalf of the fund, the adviser is not necessarily obligated to obtain the lowest possible commission cost. The adviser's obligation is to seek to obtain the most favorable terms for a transaction reasonably available under the circumstances.

The SEC has urged advisers to establish a process by which they periodically and systematically evaluate the quality and cost of services they receive from the broker-dealers with which they place client orders. The SEC staff has indicated that the factors to consider when selecting a broker-dealer, in addition to the commission and spread, may include, among other things, the broker's:

- execution, clearance, and settlement capabilities;
- financial stability;
- responsiveness to portfolio managers;
- ability to execute the transaction with minimal market price impact; and
- research capabilities, especially the value of research provided.

Directors should review the adviser's policies and procedures to ascertain whether they are reasonably designed to ensure that the funds receive best execution of portfolio trades. Directors should be especially mindful of potential conflicts when advisers allocate brokerage commissions to their affiliates. Funds may conduct brokerage transactions through an affiliated broker if those transactions are effected in compliance with Rule 17e-1 under the 1940 Act and in accordance with prescribed procedures adopted by the board (see Section 7.B(5)). There is no single way for directors to determine whether the funds are receiving best execution. Management should provide written reports that contain the names of brokers to whom they have allocated fund brokerage, the average commission rate paid, the total brokerage allocated to each firm during that period, and portfolio turnover rates. This information will assist the directors in monitoring whether brokerage allocation is consistent with the prospectus disclosure and satisfies any guidelines that directors have established. Advisers should make independent directors aware of opportunities to recapture portfolio transaction expenses for the benefit of the funds. In doing so, the directors should be satisfied that the adviser or its affiliates do not indirectly benefit from these arrangements.

An aspect of an adviser's best execution process that directors should also consider is the extent of the adviser's use of alternative trading systems in effecting portfolio transactions for a fund. Trading venues, such as "dark pools," and the use of advanced mathematical models or algorithmic trading systems, crossing networks, high frequency trading, and other alternative trading systems, are widely and increasingly used. The term "dark pool" refers to an alternative trading system that does not publicly display quotations in the consolidated market quotation system. Directors may educate themselves on developments in trading venues in a variety of ways including: (i) establishing a committee of the board to oversee in portfolio trading practices; (ii) requesting that the adviser form special committees to consider best execution and the use of client commissions and to provide reports to the board on the adviser's trading activities; (iii) requesting periodic summaries and analyses from officers of the adviser to explain the adviser's portfolio trading practices; (iv) attending trade association events, seminars and/or other education events relating to portfolio transaction execution practices; (v) subscribing to third-party information providers or retaining experts to ensure that board members remain knowledgeable with respect to market developments; and (vi) periodically meeting with portfolio managers, business unit staff, trading personnel, and other employees of the adviser to discuss these matters.

3) Soft Dollar Arrangements

Soft dollar arrangements are arrangements whereby an investment adviser obtains products or services, in addition to the execution of securities transactions, from or through a broker-dealer in exchange for the adviser directing client brokerage transactions to the broker-dealer. The products and services may be provided directly by the broker-dealer or by third parties, with the broker-dealer paying the third parties for the research. These arrangements are referred to as "soft dollars" because the adviser pays for the products and services with fund commissions rather than with cash. "Client commission arrangements" have grown to be quite common. Under a client commission arrangement, broker-dealers effecting trades for clients of an investment adviser agree to execute portfolio trades at a stated commission rate, which generally reflects an "execution only" rate, plus an additional amount that generates soft dollar credit. The amounts credited in excess of the execution only rate accumulate and can be used by the adviser to purchase a wide variety of research products. The research products may be produced by the executing broker, or by third parties.

Section 28(e) of the 1934 Act establishes a "safe harbor" for soft dollars related to brokerage and research services. The law provides that advisers with investment discretion will not be deemed to have breached their fiduciary duty to their clients solely by having the account pay more than the lowest available commission if the adviser determines in good faith that the commission is reasonable in relation to the value of brokerage and research services provided. Where an adviser engages in soft dollar practices outside the safe harbor it may be subject to liability for breaching its fiduciary duty to clients.

In 2006, the SEC published guidance that clarified its views on the scope of permitted brokerage and research services under Section 28(e). The SEC stated that products and services that have substantive content, or the expression of reasoning and knowledge, are covered under the safe harbor. Examples include market data and data services; meetings with corporate executives to obtain oral reports on company performance; attendance at conferences or seminars where substantive content is provided; and software that provides analyses of securities portfolios. Among the types of products and services not covered under the safe harbor are hardware; overhead expenses; expenses related to travel and meals when attending seminars and conferences; and mass-marketed publications.

As noted above, a fund's brokerage commissions are considered to be assets of the fund. Accordingly, an adviser's use of these commissions, including obtaining research for them, represents a potential conflict of interest. The adviser is using client assets to pay costs it may otherwise have to bear. In addition, clients of the adviser other than the fund may benefit from the research acquired with the fund's brokerage commissions. For this reason, fund directors are expected to evaluate whether the fund adviser's use of commissions is in the best interests of the fund.

In 2008, the SEC published proposed guidance for fund directors in exercising their oversight responsibilities in this area. Among other things, the SEC suggested that directors request the following types of information:

- How the adviser determines the total amount of research to be obtained, and the portion obtained through soft dollars.
- The types of research products and services to be obtained.

- The process for determining a soft dollar research budget and for allocating commission dollars. (For example, some firms utilize a vote, whereby portfolio managers and research analysts individually rate the quality of research they receive from different providers.)
- The adviser's procedures for determining that its use of soft dollars fits within the statutory safe harbor.
- How soft dollar products and services are allocated among the adviser's clients.

In addition, the SEC's release stated that fund boards should take into account soft dollar benefits received by the fund's adviser in connection with the board's annual review of the fund's advisory contract. The proposed guidance has not been finalized.

4) Trade Allocation

Directors should monitor potential conflicts arising out of allocation of trades among the adviser's various clients and as between the adviser's proprietary accounts and those of its clients. Conflicts of interest can arise particularly in situations involving initial public offerings (IPOs) or thinly traded stocks. Advisers may "bunch," or aggregate, trades of various accounts (including proprietary accounts) provided that they have established procedures designed to ensure fair allocation of trades among accounts if the trades cannot be fully executed at one time or at one price. Directors should review the procedures that advisers use to avoid, or otherwise manage properly, these conflicts to oversee that the funds are not being improperly penalized or that the advisers do not improperly benefit from their allocations.

Independent directors should not accept special investment or other opportunities, directly or indirectly, from fund advisers. In an enforcement action brought against fund directors who accepted IPO allocations, the SEC alleged that the IPO allocations were improper because they gave the directors potentially profitable opportunities that rightfully belonged to the funds and that IPO allocations to independent directors could also compromise their independence. Although directors are not prohibited from maintaining brokerage accounts with fund affiliates, they should do so only if they are treated like any other retail customer and do not receive any special treatment or opportunities. It is appropriate and customary, on the other hand, for fund directors to invest in low cost "institutional" classes of fund shares so long as such arrangements are publicly disclosed.

5) Management of Other Accounts Including Hedge Funds and Foreign Funds

Many fund advisers also provide investment advisory services to other types of clients such as unregistered private funds ("hedge funds"), off-shore funds, pension plans and other institutional clients, and high net worth investors. Management of other accounts, which may pay higher advisory fees than funds and may also pay the adviser incentive fees, alongside funds can present conflicts of interest, such as trade allocation (discussed above in Section 7.B(4)) and cross-trades.

Management of foreign funds can raise unique issues. For example, in certain foreign markets, investors and intermediaries expect to receive information regarding fund portfolio holdings that is more detailed and more frequent than is customary in the United States. Pursuant to SEC requirements, U.S. funds are required to disclose their policies and pro-cedures relating to disclosure of portfolio holdings. Such policies and procedures are intended to generally limit selective disclosure of hold-ings information. To the extent that the fund's adviser also manages off-shore funds that invest in similar securities disclosure of the offshore fund's portfolio holding could raise concerns. Directors should review how matters such as these are addressed in the fund's or the fund advis-er's compliance policies and procedures.

In addition, as part of their general oversight of the fund's adviser, directors may take an interest in any material compliance issues involv-ing other accounts that the adviser manages, such as significant issues identified in regulatory examinations.

6) Portfolio Liquidity

Guidelines previously established by the SEC staff permit an open-end fund to invest up to 15% of its net assets (10% in the case of money mar-ket funds) in illiquid assets. A security is considered illiquid if it cannot be disposed of in the ordinary course of business within seven days at approximately the value at which it appears on the fund's books. Determining the liquidity of a security is primarily an investment decision that is delegated to the investment adviser, but directors may establish guidelines and standards for determining liquidity. Determinations as to valuation and portfolio liquidity raise numerous issues for fund directors, especially in the case of restricted and other illiquid securities, Rule 144A securities (that is, privately issued securities that may be sold in secondary market transactions to qualified institutional buyers), foreign securities, and derivatives. The SEC staff guidelines, of which the portfolio liquidity standards were a part, were withdrawn in 1998 but they continue to be followed by many open-end funds.

In the wake of the 2008–2009 financial crisis, the SEC staff has emphasized liquidity "stress testing" and the role of boards in understanding funding sources of liquidity. This is especially the case for funds that invest in securities that may be thinly traded especially in times of market stress, such as high yield bonds, and for more complex funds. In 2014, the SEC announced that adoption of a liquidity management rule was a regulatory priority for 2015.

7) Securities Transactions with Affiliates

The 1940 Act contains a number of restrictions with respect to fund securities transactions involving affiliates. The four principal provisions are: (i) Section 17(a), which generally prohibits a fund from conducting principal transactions with affiliated persons; (ii) Section 10(f), which prohibits a fund from acquiring a security during the existence of an underwriting or selling syndicate relating to that security in which an affiliated person is acting as a member; (iii) Section 17(e), which regulates brokerage or agency transactions by a fund with affiliated persons; and (iv) Section 17(d) and Rule 17d-1 thereunder, which prohibit an affiliated person acting as principal from engaging in certain transactions in which the fund is a joint or joint and several participant.

The SEC has adopted exemptive rules relating to these provisions that set forth specific responsibilities for the independent directors. Each of these exemptive rules is premised on the responsibility of the independent directors to adopt and monitor the implementation of certain prescribed procedures to mitigate the effects of the inherent conflicts of interest in portfolio transactions involving affiliates.

8) Securities Lending

Many funds lend their portfolio securities through securities lending programs administered by banks or broker-dealers. Securities lending is the practice of lending securities to another party in exchange for a fee or a share of income on the investment of collateral for the loaned securities. Borrowers, such as broker-dealers and private funds, use securities borrowed from the lender to implement specific investment strategies, such as facilitating short sales of securities. Many different kinds of portfolio securities can be loaned.

A fund typically receives cash or U.S. government securities as collateral for the loaned securities. Cash collateral is typically reinvested in short-term, high-quality investments in order to provide maximum liquidity to pay back the borrower when it returns the loaned securities. The fee paid by a borrower takes the form of a portion of the earnings from the investment of the cash collateral. A portion of the earnings is shared with the borrower in the form of a rebate, and a portion is shared with the securities lending agent in exchange for its services. For non-cash collateral, the lender receives a fee or premium for the loan of securities. As a practical matter, a fund earns a higher return in the case of loaned securities that are in high demand. The borrower will either receive a lower rebate or pay higher fees.

Many funds use a securities lending agent to select and monitor borrowers, help select securities to be loaned, and negotiate and effect loan agreements with the borrowers. The portion of the earnings on the cash collateral that is paid to the lending agent is commonly referred to as a "fee split." The bank administering the securities lending program acts as lending agent, and is often the fund's custodian as well.

The SEC staff permits funds to loan their portfolio securities provided that, among other things, the fund receives collateral from the borrower in an amount at least equal to the value of the borrowed securities. In addition, the borrowed securities must be marked to market daily and the borrower must post additional collateral as necessary to meet that requirement. At any given time, a fund may only lend one-third of its total assets, which calculation can include the collateral received, and the fund must be able to recall its loans at any time. Securities lending also implicates shareholder disclosure requirements of the 1940 Act and proxy voting requirements. Finally, the SEC staff expects a fund to receive a reasonable return on the loan, due to the risk to which the fund's assets are exposed. Fund directors should be satisfied that they understand these risks and how they are mitigated (which may include indemnification arrangements with the securities lending agent) and disclosed to investors.

The SEC staff has directed a role for a fund's board with respect to securities lending. In essence, the staff expects a fund's board to approve the fund's participation in a program, including the contract with the securities lending agent, and the amount of the fees to be paid by the fund. The amount of the fees paid to the securities lending agent relates directly to whether participation in the program is in the best interests of a fund, as those fees diminish the return to the fund. Similarly, the type of investment of the cash collateral is a decision for the board of directors and should not be delegated to anyone other than the investment adviser. As a general matter, the board should understand the basis upon which the fund meets the specific regulatory aspects that are noted above, such as the ability to recall securities that are "out on loan" for purposes of voting proxies, as well as for portfolio management purposes. Many funds invest cash collateral in affiliated money market funds. In evaluating such arrangements, directors must recognize that fund advisers have a conflict of interest in recommending them, and be satisfied that they are in the best interests of the fund after considering alternatives. As with all fund activities, a fund board has general oversight responsibilities with respect to a fund's participation in a securities lending program.

As a practical matter, the board of a fund that engages in securities lending should evaluate the risks associated with securities lending and understand how the investment adviser and securities lending agent identify, monitor, and mitigate the risks. Many boards receive periodic reports from fund management (or the lending agent) about the program, which allow the board to review the returns from participation in the program, the degree to which a fund participates in the program, and information about the kinds of securities that are on loan.

Additional regulatory requirements apply to a fund's use of an affiliated person as the securities lending agent (such as a bank that is affiliated with the fund's investment adviser). Those "affiliated lending programs" require additional oversight by a fund's board. The board of a fund that uses an affiliated securities lending agent could work with the fund's CCO to establish appropriate procedures to help ensure compliance with the applicable regulatory guidelines and the conditions of any exemptive order.

9) Certain Special Types of Investment Practices

The SEC requires directors to make certain inquiries when funds engage in (i) repurchase agreements, (ii) reverse repurchase agreements, forward commitments and similar arrangements and (iii) transactions in options, futures contracts, options on future contracts, forward contracts and other derivative strategies. These inquiries should focus on the strategies being pursued, the scope of their use, the risks involved, the creditworthiness of counterparties, any valuation issues and whether the practices are being conducted in a safe and sound manner. (See Section 10 for information as to the director's duties to monitor a fund's use of derivatives.)

10) Leverage

With the rising use of alternative investment strategies by registered funds, leverage plays an increasing role in many fund portfolios. While potentially a powerful tool for advisers in pursuing a fund's investment objective, the use of leverage can involve significant risk, and is subject to legal restrictions under the 1940 Act and SEC interpretations. Effective board oversight of a fund that utilizes leverage requires a broad understanding of how leverage is obtained and fits into the fund's investment strategy, as well as the steps taken by the adviser and the fund's CCO to ensure compliance with applicable regulatory requirements and fund policies.

Generally speaking, leverage involves the use of debt or other instruments to increase the fund's investment exposures, thereby boosting potential returns at the cost of increased risk of loss as well as explicit or implicit financing charges. Explicit leverage involves the issuance of indebtedness by a fund. By borrowing cash and investing the proceeds, a fund amplifies the potential return, and risk, to its investors. However, leverage can also be achieved implicitly through the use of derivatives, reverse repurchase agreements, firm and standby commitment agreements and other techniques, some of which are complex. For example, in exchange for the small up-front cost of entering into a futures contract, a fund may gain exposure to the full change in price of a very large position, e.g., in underlying bonds or a foreign currency, without having any ownership interest in the assets underlying the contract. In its leveraging effect on the fund, entering into a derivative contract can be very similar to buying the underlying security on credit. (For a discussion of derivatives more generally, see Section 10.)

Section 18 of the 1940 Act imposes significant restrictions on the use of leverage by funds. Open-end funds are prohibited from issuing "senior securities," but may borrow only from banks, subject to asset coverage requirements. Closed-end funds are granted greater flexibility, and may issue specified types of senior securities subject to asset coverage and other requirements. (See Section 13 for a discussion of considerations specific to closed-end funds.)

On its face Section 18 refers to explicit indebtedness. Under SEC staff interpretations, however, it also imposes limitations on an open-end fund's ability to enter into transactions creating implicit leverage. While open-end funds are not prohibited from engaging in such transactions outright, the fund must "cover" the risk resulting from such a transaction by either entering into an offsetting transaction or maintaining a segregated account with sufficient liquid assets to satisfy its obligations under the transaction.

Under the compliance program rule (Rule 38a-1), funds must have in place written policies and procedures reasonably designed to ensure compliance with the federal securities laws. Accordingly, funds should have established policies designed to ensure compliance with Section 18, including policies to address coverage procedures with respect to derivative and other transactions that have the effect of leveraging a fund's portfolio.

C. Other Specific Statutory and Regulatory Responsibilities

Directors have specific responsibilities under the 1940 Act with respect to approval of a number of other matters besides advisory and distribution arrangements and the matters discussed in Section 7.A and B, including custody arrangements, fidelity bonds and joint insurance policies, selection of independent accountants, codes of ethics and other matters described below. See Appendix A for a list of significant matters in this regard. Counsel normally provides the directors with guidance in meeting their specific responsibilities.

1) Custody Arrangements

The 1940 Act requires that the securities of a fund be maintained in the custody of a qualified custodian. The directors have a duty to oversee the fund's custody arrangements. In addition, directors have specific obligations for monitoring certain types of custody arrangements, including the use of self-custody or affiliated custody arrangements, and foreign custody arrangements. Of particular importance are Rules 17f-5 and 17f-7 (which permit a fund to maintain its foreign securities with a foreign custodian or a foreign depository). Rules 17f-5 and 17f-7 permit directors to delegate responsibility for the selection of foreign sub-custodians and the monitoring of both these sub-custodians and foreign securities depositories. These rules contain specific conditions and require consideration of a number of factors and specific findings by the board of directors.

2) Fidelity Bonds and Joint Insurance Policies

Rule 17g-1 under the 1940 Act requires each fund to maintain a bond against larceny and embezzlement and requires that the independent directors approve the form and amount of the bond. A fund can purchase fidelity bond coverage jointly with other funds and their investment adviser and distributor and certain other persons so long as the independent directors approve the allocation of the premium to each particular fund after consideration of certain specified factors.

Funds also often acquire either or both (i) errors and omissions insurance to cover losses from negligent acts of persons acting on behalf of a fund for which the fund might be held responsible and/or (ii) director and officer liability insurance to cover amounts recovered against a fund's directors and officers and amounts paid by the fund to indemnify its directors and officers. Such policies also cover the costs of defending any claims brought against the fund, its directors or officers. Such insurance may be purchased jointly with a fund adviser, underwriter or other affiliate if the fund's directors, including a majority of the independent directors, approve the arrangement annually after making certain specified findings. Any such joint policy may not exclude coverage for litigation between the adviser and the independent directors. The policy should allow for advancement of expenses if an action is brought against the directors. The policy also should be structured on a "several" basis so that, if one insured person is disqualified from coverage, the remaining insured are still protected. In recent years, some funds have purchased supplemental liability insurance with policy limits reserved for the independent directors (see Section 16.D).

3) Selection of Independent Accountants

The 1940 Act requires a fund's independent accountant to be selected for each fiscal year at an in-person meeting by a majority of the fund's independent directors. The 1940 Act provides that selection of independent accountants must be submitted for ratification or rejection by fund shareholders at the next annual meeting of shareholders (if the fund holds such a meeting). Rule 32a-4 under the 1940 Act exempts investment companies from this shareholder approval requirement if the fund has an audit committee composed entirely of independent directors and the audit committee has adopted a written charter. In selecting fund accountants, the directors should consider the qualifications, reputation, and independence of the proposed accountants, the identity and skill of the engagement team assigned to the fund and the proposed scope of the audit and fees. (See Section 4.B(1) for information as to the duties imposed by the Sarbanes-Oxley Act on the audit committee as to the independent accountants.)

4) Codes of Ethics

Section 17(j) of the 1940 Act and Rule 17j-1 require that investment companies, their investment advisers and principal underwriters adopt and enforce codes of ethics reasonably designed to prevent "access persons" from defrauding the investment company with respect to purchases or sales of securities. Access persons of a fund include its directors and officers and certain advisory and underwriter personnel. To the extent a fund's independent directors have no actual knowledge of the fund's trading in specific securities, those directors are generally exempt from most aspects of the fund's code of ethics. Codes of ethics generally require reporting of securities transactions by access persons, prohibit certain types of transactions, and require preclearance of certain trades. Procedures reasonably designed to prevent violations should be reviewed on a regular basis to help ensure that they are adequate to enforce the standards of conduct that are contained in the codes of ethics. In addition, directors should be familiar with the applicable codes of ethics of their funds' sub-advisers and other service providers and monitor their effectiveness. Boards, including a majority of the independent directors, must approve the codes of ethics of the fund, each investment adviser and the principal underwriter of the fund, and any material changes to the codes, after receiving specified certifications and making a determination that the codes contain provisions reasonably designed to prevent access persons from violating the codes. Boards receive reports at least annually of any significant violations of the codes and of the sanctions, if any, that are imposed, as well as certifications that procedures are in place to prevent violations.

Funds must disclose whether they have adopted a code of ethics contemplated by the Sarbanes-Oxley Act that covers their principal executive officers and senior financial officers and, if not, an explanation of why they have not done so. The Sarbanes-Oxley Act code of ethics addresses a broader range of ethical conduct than the Rule 17j-1 code. Issues to be addressed include: (i) the handling of conflicts of interest between personal and professional relationships; (ii) full, fair, and accurate filings with the SEC; and (iii) compliance with applicable laws and regulations. Although it is not required, the Sarbanes-Oxley Act-mandated code of ethics can be integrated with the code required under Rule 17j-1.

Each director must strictly comply with the applicable provisions of the code of ethics of the fund. Directors should seek advice of counsel before accepting special investment opportunities or other benefits from anyone associated with the fund or the investment adviser, such as purchases of securities in initial public offerings and private placements.

Mutual funds must disclose in their registration statements their policies and procedures with respect to the disclosure of their portfolio securities and any ongoing arrangements to make available information about their portfolio securities. Directors should monitor the effectiveness of these procedures.

5) *Fund Names*

Section 35(d) of the 1940 Act prohibits funds from using misleading names, and Rule 35d-1 thereunder requires a fund with a name suggesting that it focuses on a particular type of investment, industry, or geographic locale to invest, under normal circumstances, at least 80% of its net assets (plus any borrowings for investment purposes) in that investment, industry, or locale. The directors should keep this requirement in mind when reviewing the fund's investment portfolio.

6) *Anti-money Laundering*

The USA PATRIOT Act of 2001 requires that financial institutions, including investment companies, adopt anti-money laundering ("AML") programs designed to make it easier to prevent, detect, and prosecute international money laundering and terrorist financing activities. As part of such required AML programs, funds must adopt procedures to verify the identities of their investors and keep records of such verification. Mutual funds are also required to report suspicious activity similar to the suspicious activity reports required of banks and broker-dealers. A fund's AML program must be approved by the fund's board of directors. The board should periodically assess the effectiveness of a fund's AML program and implementing procedures as well as receive reports from the designated AML compliance officer responsible for monitoring the program. A fund may delegate certain aspects of AML program implementation to service providers but remains responsible for general oversight and conduct of the AML program.

7) *Privacy Procedures*

Under Regulation S-P, the SEC requires mutual funds to follow procedures designed to prevent the funds from sharing personal information about their shareholders with unaffiliated third parties. Many mutual funds also are subject to an SEC rule requiring anti-identity theft procedures. The board should monitor the funds' compliance with these requirements. (See Section 7.C(10) for a discussion about privacy and anti-identity theft procedures in the context of cybersecurity.)

8) Insider Trading

There may be times when investment advisers, in the course of managing fund assets, obtain material, nonpublic information about an issuer of securities. Insiders, including fund directors, are prohibited from purchasing or selling securities when they possess material, nonpublic information about the issuer and from "tipping" or disclosing such information to others who may use it in trading. Giving others recommendations to buy or sell while in possession of such information is also prohibited.

Although fund directors are privy to a wide array of information about their funds, they normally do not have access to the type of inside information usually available to directors of business corporations. Nonetheless, they may become privy to nonpublic information with respect to the fund itself or with respect to issuers of portfolio securities, such as information pertaining to a prospective tender offer or to a bankrupt issuer.

Purchasing or selling securities based upon this kind of confidential information, or merely passing the information on to someone else who acts on that information, is illegal. Insider trading may result in criminal prosecution and disgorgement of profits, fines, and other sanctions in actions instituted by the SEC. Directors should exercise caution that information learned through their service as officers or directors of public companies is not improperly communicated to the fund and its affiliates.

In some cases, advisers may adopt procedures designed to create a firewall between the portfolio personnel who may have access to inside information and other personnel in the fund complex.

Directors of funds whose activities could result in adviser personnel receiving inside information—for example, when serving on a creditors' committee in a bankruptcy proceeding—should satisfy themselves that the adviser has adequate procedures to prevent the misuse of such information as part of their monitoring of investment practices.

9) Business Continuity Plan

Funds and their service providers should maintain comprehensive and viable business continuity plans in the event of large-scale disruptions in the fund's operations and those of its adviser and other service providers. The plans should be designed to achieve maximum business continuity in the event of a variety of contingencies, including long-term major disruptions. The plans must be reviewed and updated continuously. The directors should be informed periodically of the business continuity program and should consider its adequacy. (See Section 7.C(10) for a discussion about business continuity plans in the context of cybersecurity.)

10) Cybersecurity

With enhancements in new technology, increasing sophistication of cyber attacks and the increasing popularity and use of cloud computing services, directors should review whether a fund and its service providers have adequate cybersecurity policies, procedures and protections in place. In overseeing policies and procedures relating to cybersecurity, boards should consider whether a fund's and its service providers' policies and procedures are reasonably designed to prevent violations of the federal securities laws in accordance with Rule 38a-1 under the 1940 Act (see Section 9). Boards should focus on personal identifying information of investors held by a fund or its agents, an adviser's risk management, incident management, use of technology, and vendor access and due diligence.

The nature of board reports on cybersecurity will likely vary by firm as there is no one-size-fits-all approach. Boards should be mindful of how such reporting may need to evolve over time.

Certain federal securities laws require funds or their service providers to adopt policies and procedures relating, in part, to cybersecurity. For example, Regulation S-P (relating to customer privacy) requires that funds have policies and procedures that address safeguards for the protection of customer information. The Identity Theft "Red Flags" Rule, which also has implications for cybersecurity, requires boards to approve a red flags identity theft protection program. An organization's red flags program should, among other things, be appropriately tailored to the organization's size and complexity, designed to identify relevant patterns, practices, or specific activities that indicate possible identity theft, or "red flags"; and respond appropriately to any red flags detected. The red flags program should be updated from time to time to reflect changes in risks from identity theft. Boards may also wish to consider how a cyber breach could impact a fund's safeguarding of the integrity of its records and financial reporting and the custody of fund assets.

In addition, boards should review with fund service providers the business continuity plans they have in place to respond to cyber attacks. One area of cyber attacks that boards should focus on is the adviser's ability to defend against so-called "distributed denial-of-service attacks," which are attacks designed to disable website functionality. If shareholders in a fund complex are permitted to redeem shares online, such an attack may impose a significant burden on a shareholder's ability to do so, thereby compromising the exercise of a shareholder right to redeem open-end fund shares mandated in the 1940 Act.

Boards may also wish to review with fund service providers the following areas, among others: any insurance coverage that would apply to cyber breaches; the service providers' breach response plans; how the service providers' cyber protections compare to industry practices; and oversight of third-party vendors that have access to key information about the fund or its shareholders.

In reviewing and approving policies and procedures relating to cybersecurity, directors should consider their fiduciary duties under state law and their role with respect to the oversight of risk management, and the regulatory and reputational risks to funds from inadequate cybersecurity protections. There are a myriad of risks attendant with inadequate cybersecurity, such as negative media attention, debilitating cyber attacks, SEC enforcement actions, and inappropriate release of shareholder information or the adviser's proprietary trading information.

11) Social Media

Social media offers multiple potential business applications, including advertising and marketing, providing customer service to shareholders, and broadcasting live events. With respect to social media, it is helpful for directors to understand the primary purpose(s) for which a fund complex or an adviser uses social media in order to understand the nature of risks that may present themselves.

Both FINRA and the SEC have published guidance for fund distributors and advisers, respectively that recommends the adoption of social media policies and procedures. As addressed in Section 9, Rule 38a-1 requires a finding by the board that the funds' and certain service providers' policies and procedures are reasonably designed to prevent violations of the federal securities laws. The SEC's guidance on social media recommends that firms should adopt, and periodically review the effectiveness of, social media policies and procedures. FINRA and SEC guidance encourages firms to adopt specific social media policies, rather than relying on multiple overlapping policies, inasmuch as the firms' existing advertising and marketing policies may not accurately and consistently address the unique risks presented by social media communications. Existing rules governing communications, such as antifraud provisions, the prohibition on testimonials, and rules relating to suitability, recordkeeping and information security also apply. Given that social media is a fast-evolving form of communication, firms that utilize social media also need to be prepared to make judgments in areas not addressed by FINRA and SEC guidance.

In reviewing and approving policies and procedures relating to social media, directors should consider their fiduciary duties under state law and their role with respect to the oversight of risk management, and the regulatory and reputational risks to funds from the use of social media. While a social media presence can be used to help develop a fund complex's brand, similar to cybersecurity risks, social media use could dilute or damage that brand if used inappropriately or not monitored carefully. Fund firms may be at risk if social media programs do not provide for appropriate training and supervision of employees permitted to engage in social media for business purposes, including the risk of enforcement actions by FINRA or the SEC.

12) Whistleblower Program

The Dodd-Frank Act mandated that the SEC establish a whistleblower program designed to incentivize individuals to provide the SEC with specific, credible, and timely information about possible securities law violations and to provide monetary awards to individuals furnishing such information under certain conditions. This Act contains anti-retaliation provisions designed to protect any "whistleblower." This program is administered by the Office of Whistleblower ("OWB"), which operates as a separate office within the SEC's Division of Enforcement.

13) Market Timing

A significant part of the mutual fund trading abuses in the early 2000s involved market timing, late trading, and selective disclosure of portfolio information. As a result of reforms implemented in response to these abuses, mutual funds must describe in their prospectuses the risks, if any, that frequent purchases and redemptions of fund shares may present for other shareholders of the funds. The prospectus must also state whether the directors have adopted policies and procedures with respect to frequent purchases and redemptions of shares by fund shareholders. If the board has not adopted any such policies and procedures, the prospectus must include a statement of the specific basis for the view of the board that it is appropriate for the fund not to have such policies and procedures. If the board has adopted such policies and procedures, the fund's prospectus must include a detailed description of those policies and procedures addressing an extensive number of factors. Among the factors, there must be a description of procedures designed to restrict market timing and the extent to which these restrictions have not been imposed. There also must be a description of any arrangements with any person to permit market timing.

D. Role of the Board in Special Situations

Mutual funds are susceptible to extraordinary or emergency situations as a result of their constant exposure to securities markets and their daily obligations with respect to the sale and redemption of their shares. The types of extraordinary or emergency situations are limited only by the imagination. A problem could affect the entire industry, a portion of the industry or just an individual fund or fund complex. An example of an industry-wide event would be a computer failure on a major trading facility. A severe weather disaster in a particular region of the country may affect funds with critical service providers in that region when, for example, it results in a widespread power outage, and backup arrangements fail, complicating the proper handling of purchase and redemption orders. On the other hand, the failure of a fund complex computer system would affect only the funds in that complex. A flood of redemption requests, generated by news or rumor, might exceed a fund's capacity to handle the situation. An employee, by means of false entries (for example, forged redemption requests) may have embezzled millions of dollars.

Response to an emergency situation will depend in large measure upon the nature of the problem. The independent directors should monitor whether fund management has contingency plans in place so that appropriate measures can be taken on an expedited basis in response to matters that may arise and so that all significant persons and entities involved in fund management and operations can be, and are, quickly informed. Depending upon the situation, a telephonic or in-person meeting of the directors with fund management and counsel may be appropriate. Situations that place the fund and its manager in an adversarial position increase the need for the independent directors to consult their own legal counsel, and potentially other advisors.

In addition to notification of directors, fund counsel and fund personnel, certain situations (such as an inability to satisfy redemption requests) may also require immediate notification of the SEC staff and fund shareholders. Where a problem is industry-wide, or affects a sizeable fund population, the SEC will quickly become aware of the problem, and the resolution will most likely be uniform for all affected funds. In that situation, the primary responsibility of fund management is to keep current with developments and be ready to act in accordance with them.

The relative importance of the matter will determine when or whether shareholders should be notified.

1) Statutory, Regulatory, and Related Problems or Violations

The independent directors may be confronted with a situation involving a statutory, regulatory or other violation on the part of the fund. Examples include the making of prohibited investments, the engaging in prohibited affiliated transactions, the failure to observe investment restrictions or sales practice violations. Many fund advisers have error correction policies that require them to put a fund in at least as good a position as if the error had not occurred, but errors or violations may involve multiple service providers and the responsibility for, and potential resolution of, some situations may not be clear cut. Resolution of the matter may require negotiation with the investment adviser, the distributor or some other service provider responsible for the matter. Under these circumstances, the independent directors should consider consulting with legal counsel that is independent of the service provider involved and such other advisors as they deem appropriate. Resolution of the matter may involve negotiating some form of settlement or corrective action with the responsible entity and determining whether the relevant regulatory authorities and shareholders should be notified of the problem and the manner in which it was resolved.

Independent directors should clearly establish with fund management that the directors expect to be promptly notified of any statutory, regulatory, or related problems or violations.

2) Mergers and Liquidations

The term "merger" in the mutual fund context is typically used to refer to the acquisition by a fund of the assets and liabilities of another fund in exchange for shares of the acquiring fund, which are distributed to the shareholders of the acquired fund. Mergers are common in the mutual fund industry. Directors are typically responsible for approving these transactions under state law. Where affiliated mergers are concerned, the independent directors also have specific responsibilities under the 1940 Act with respect to their approval.

Mergers may involve the combinations of two or more existing funds, or the merging of an existing fund(s) into a newly created shell fund that is part of another fund complex (often called a "shell reorganization"). Mergers may be proposed for a variety of reasons. For example, where a fund has had poor investment performance or is not economically viable, a merger with a better performing or larger fund may be proposed. Fund mergers may also be proposed where two investment management firms have merged or one firm has acquired another, resulting in overlapping products in the fund line-up. Combining such similar funds could result in administrative efficiencies, and potential expense savings or economies of scale for the funds and/or the adviser. Mergers are typically structured so as to be tax-free, and often are contingent upon delivery of an opinion of counsel to that effect.

Under state corporate law, the approval of the board of directors of the acquired fund and the approval of the board of directors of the acquiring fund are typically required. In deciding whether to approve a transaction, directors should consider whether the transaction is in the best interests of the fund, keeping in mind their duty of loyalty and care, as discussed in Section 3.A.

Rule 17a-8 allows mergers of affiliated funds, which would otherwise be prohibited as an affiliated transaction under Section 17 of the 1940 Act. Under this rule, the board of directors must request and evaluate information reasonably necessary to make required determinations. In order to rely on Rule 17a-8 for an affiliated merger, the directors of each fund, including a majority of the independent directors, must determine that the transaction is in the best interests of the fund and that the interests of the shareholders of the fund will not be diluted. Specifically, the following factors, in addition to any other relevant information, should be considered: (i) any fees or expenses that will be borne directly or indirectly by the fund in connection with the merger, (ii) any effect of the merger on annual fund operating expenses and shareholder fees and services, (iii) any change in the fund's investment objectives, restrictions, and policies that will result from the merger, and (iv) any direct or indirect federal income tax consequences of the merger to fund shareholders. Other relevant factors may include consideration in any differences in the nature and quality of distribution services, class structure, fund performance, transaction costs and potential tax consequences of repositioning the fund's portfolio, board composition, and any other aspect of the transaction that could impact the combined fund. The directors of the acquired fund may seek assurances that the acquired fund has no undisclosed or unaccrued liabilities, such as tax liabilities. In addition, the board should consider whether any alternatives to the merger, including continuation of the fund, its liquidation or other potential transactions may be in the best interests of the fund. The board may also consider the costs of the merger and who will bear those costs (i.e., the fund or the adviser). If the adviser is expected to benefit from cost savings relating to the merger, it is not unusual for the adviser to bear all or some of the merger expenses (including the costs of a proxy solicitation, if required). The weight to attribute to each of these factors is a matter within the business judgment of the board.

Under Rule 17a-8, shareholder approval of the acquired fund is required unless (i) no fundamental investment restrictions will be changed, (ii) there is no material difference in the advisory contract, except for the identity of the fund parties to the contract, (iii) the independent directors of the acquired fund will comprise a majority of the directors of the acquiring fund, and (iv) any distribution fees of the acquiring fund are no greater than the distribution fees authorized to be paid by the acquired fund. It is important to keep in mind, however, that even if shareholder approval is not required under Rule 17a-8, state law or the fund's organizational documents may require shareholder approval of the acquired fund and/or the acquiring fund. In addition, for closed-end funds, exchange rules may require shareholder approval.

If the merger is in connection with the sale of advisory business, which results in the assignment of an advisory agreement as discussed in Section 5.F of this Guidebook, Section 15(f) of the 1940 Act permits the adviser of an acquired fund to benefit from the sale, provided that the board of the combined fund maintains a certain level of independence for three years after the sale of the adviser's business (at least 75% of the combined fund's board is comprised of directors who are not "interested persons" of the adviser or its predecessor) and the transaction does not place an unfair burden on shareholders. An "unfair burden" would include any arrangement during the two-year period after the transaction whereby the adviser or any "interested person" of the adviser receives or is entitled to receive any compensation other than for *bona fide* investment advisory or other services. As a result, boards typically evaluate whether the expense ratio of the acquired fund will be at or below the expense ratio of the acquiring fund for the two-year period following the merger. Compliance with Section 15(f) is not required; rather, the section is viewed as a "safe harbor."

Liquidation is also considered for funds from time to time, particularly for smaller funds that may not be economically viable. Directors should consider the tax consequences of liquidating in that, unlike most mergers, liquidations typically result in a taxable distribution with shareholders' recognizing capital gains/losses. They may also result in the permanent loss of tax loss carryforwards. Nevertheless, liquidation may be appropriate where a merger candidate is not available or appropriate. In approving a liquidation, the directors typically will be asked to approve a plan of liquidation, and should request information regarding how the process of liquidating the fund's assets will be conducted, estimated time frame, anticipated cash distributions to investors and tax consequences for shareholders. In addition to board approval, some liquidations may require approval of the liquidating fund's shareholders depending on the requirements under applicable state law requirements and/or the fund's organizational documents.

In connection with a merger or liquidation, directors should consider potential liabilities of the affected funds and where the risk of such liabilities may fall. For example, directors should consider whether the acquiring fund in a merger will acquire all liabilities of the acquired fund or just certain stated liabilities. If not all liabilities are acquired the directors of the acquired fund must be satisfied that they are duly provided for.

Directors may also wish to consider whether to obtain "tail coverage" or other indemnification or insurance for funds that may be merged or liquidated as the assets of the funds and existing insurance coverage may no longer be available to provide indemnification/insurance to the directors. (See Section 16 for further discussion of indemnification and insurance.)

Board's Responsibility for Valuation

A. Net Asset Value Determination

Fund net asset value ("NAV") determinations are of particular importance for open-end management investment companies because all transactions in fund shares—purchases, redemptions and exchanges—are processed at the NAV next determined after the transaction order is placed. Such determinations are also relevant for exchange-traded funds, which also determine NAVs on a daily basis, and for exchange-traded closed-end management investment companies, which as a matter of market convention calculate and publish NAVs on a daily basis. Closed-end funds that are listed on exchanges are also required to compute and publish their NAV periodically, and such NAV is important to stockholders in valuing their investment and is used for various purposes including fee calculations and reinvestment of distributions. For open-end funds and certain closed-end funds transacting at NAV, errors in valuation can lead to costly adjustments and, to the extent that shareholders suffer any material loss, the party responsible for the error likely will be required to reimburse the fund and its shareholders. While most secondary market transactions in fund shares for ETFs and closed-end funds are based on market price rather than NAV, accurate NAV determination is crucial to analyzing premium/discount data for such funds. In addition, because asset-based payments, such as most advisory fees, are accrued based upon NAV, it is critical that fund assets be valued on a fair and accurate basis.

B. Board's Fair Value Obligation

Boards have a statutory obligation in the 1940 Act to determine the "fair value" of fund portfolio securities for which market quotations are not readily available. The SEC has taken the position that this duty is not delegable. However, day-to-day aspects of the valuation process may be performed by third parties, subject to oversight by the board.

The board should approve the valuation methodologies used in establishing the daily values of the fund's assets and monitor the accuracy with which fair valuations are carried out. Portfolio securities must be valued at market prices in the case of securities for which market quotations are readily available. When market prices are not readily available, such as when trading is suspended or when the fund holds restricted or other illiquid securities, including certain over-the-counter derivative instruments, the securities must be valued at fair value, determined in good faith by the directors. There also may be times when there are questions as to the reliability of market quotations in which case it may be inappropriate to consider the closing prices as "readily available," and fair value pricing should be used.

The directors of an open-end fund must determine the specific time or times of the day at which the fund computes its NAV per share. While most funds compute their NAV as of the close of the New York Stock Exchange, some funds have selected different times of the day for special reasons and others compute NAV more frequently than once a day.

The approaches and appropriate procedures for valuation may vary based on the type of fund and instrument involved. For example, funds holding securities traded on foreign exchanges may have special valuation issues resulting from the fact that the foreign markets may operate at times that do not coincide with the major U.S. markets, resulting in the closing prices of foreign portfolio securities being many hours old at the time of the funds' NAV calculation. If a significant event affecting the value of securities has occurred in this interim period, the fund should consider using fair-value pricing rather than the last available market quotation. This can, among other things, prevent short-term investors in mutual funds from exploiting price discrepancies that have arisen. Many funds have engaged third party service providers to use proprietary models to fair value foreign securities daily or when triggered by specified daily percentage changes in U.S. markets.

There is no straightforward definition for what it means for a security to be valued at "fair value," and no single method for determining what a security's fair value is. Guidance from the SEC and the Financial Accounting Standards Board has provided some general principles as to what fair value means. Based on that guidance, a security's fair value on a given day is what a fund can reasonably expect to receive for that security if it were to sell the security that day in the ordinary course (i.e., not a "fire sale" in a distressed situation). There is no expectation that different funds will necessarily arrive at the same price when determining a security's fair value (though it is generally expected that if two funds in a single complex hold the same security, the security will be valued the same for each fund).

In practice, there are several ways in which a fund's board can discharge its duty to determine the fair value of the securities in the fund's portfolio in good faith. Typically, a board establishes processes to oversee the valuation function and tasks a third party with the day-to-day mechanics of valuation, almost always the fund's adviser or administrator. SEC guidance expressly permits this arrangement, so long as it is pursuant to the board's direction and oversight.

C. Valuation Policies and Procedures

When tasking a third party with day-to-day valuation functions, the SEC has expressed its expectation that a fund's valuation policies will have clear and specific valuation methodologies for specific portfolio assets or classes of assets. In addition, in adopting Rule 38a-1, the SEC stated that a fund must adopt written policies and procedures to monitor for circumstances that may necessitate the use of fair value prices; establish criteria for determining when market quotations are no longer reliable for a particular portfolio security; provide a methodology by which the fund determines the current fair value of the portfolio security; and regularly review the appropriateness and accuracy of the method used in valuing securities and make any necessary adjustments. Practices regarding board review, approval and/or ratification of valuations not determined pursuant to a board-approved methodology vary. Funds must disclose in their prospectuses both the circumstances under which they will use fair value pricing and the effects of using fair value pricing.

The SEC has stated that the criteria used for determining when fair value pricing must be used is an area that deserves close scrutiny by fund directors. The Division of Investment Management maintains a bibliography on its website of the SEC's published guidance relating to the valuation of portfolio securities and other assets held by registered investment companies (www.sec.gov/divisions/investment/icvaluation.htm).

Although the SEC has expressly stated that the board may appoint others, such as the fund's investment adviser or a valuation committee, to assist it in determining fair value, and to make the actual calculations pursuant to the fair valuation methodologies previously approved by the directors, such an arrangement is subject to an additional requirement that the board oversees the policies in good faith. The SEC has said that a board acts in good faith when it continuously reviews the appropriateness of the method used to determine the fair value of the fund's portfolio securities, referencing the duties of care and loyalty the directors owe the fund (see Section 3). Conversely, the SEC has stated that a board is not acting in good faith if it knows or has reason to believe that its fair value determination does not reflect the amount that might reasonably be expected to be received by the fund on a current sale, or if it acts with reckless disregard to whether its value determinations meet the fair value standard described above.

In approving written policies in good faith, boards should approve specific valuation methodologies used to value portfolio securities after having acquired a sufficient understanding of the proposed methodologies. For example, a fund's valuation methodologies might include using evaluated prices from a specified pricing service to establish the fair value of certain types of securities (e.g., debt securities) or using amortized cost for debt securities with remaining maturities of 60 days or less. Because the decision to use a third-party pricing service is viewed by the SEC staff as approving a fair valuation methodology, the board should review the appropriateness of the methodologies used by the pricing service. Again, the board may appoint others to assist it with this review.

The SEC has stated, including in the SEC's July 2014 release adopting money market fund reform (applicable to all funds), that, before deciding to use evaluated prices from a pricing service to assist in fair valuation, the board may want to consider the inputs, methods, models and assumptions used by the pricing service and how those inputs, methods, models and assumptions are affected (if at all) as market conditions change. The SEC has further stated that boards may want to assess the quality of the evaluated prices provided by the pricing service and the extent to which the evaluated prices are determined as close as possible to the time as of which the fund calculates its NAV. Most directors are not valuation experts and, with regard to the foregoing, they may receive assistance from the investment adviser or administrator or other party to which certain valuation responsibilities have been delegated, and may choose to meet with certain key pricing service representatives at periodic intervals. Regarding the use of amortized cost, the SEC has stated that generally a fund may only use amortized cost when it can reasonably conclude, each time a valuation determination is made, that the amortized cost value of the portfolio security is approximately the same as the fair value of the security as determined without amortized cost.

After methodologies are established and incorporated into written policies, boards should review valuations for their continuing adequacy by receiving reports from the investment adviser or administrator or other party the board has tasked with certain valuation responsibilities. In this regard, boards should consider the usefulness of back-testing, such as comparisons of sale prices to valuations used immediately prior to sale. Boards also should oversee the process by which fund service providers are monitoring "stale" prices (valuations that are unchanged for a period of days), pricing service "overrides" (rejection of a pricing service price in favor of a different price when the pricing service price is determined to be inaccurate) and price challenges (a pricing service's price is challenged and whether the challenges are typically higher or lower than the original price provided). Some boards find it helpful to receive periodic reports on such monitoring. As part of their ongoing oversight of pricing matters, boards should review and approve changes to pricing policies and procedures, and many boards review such policies and procedures at least annually regardless of whether changes are proposed.

To the extent valuations are determined other than pursuant to a pre-approved methodology (such as when neither market price nor an evaluated price from pricing service price is available), boards should review such valuation determinations to fulfill their statutory responsibility for valuation. In connection with this review, boards should receive all information reasonably necessary to understand the determinations. Boards also may wish to consider process matters in valuation determinations, such as the role of portfolio managers, who may be deemed to have a conflict of interest and bias in favor of higher valuations, in determining valuations but who nonetheless may be the most knowledgeable about a particular security. In addition, boards should keep in mind that the SEC indicated in the settlement discussed below with the Morgan Keegan funds directors that boards cannot simply rely on routine financial statement audits by independent registered public accounting firms for valuation assurance, so boards should understand the assurances, or lack thereof, provided by the pricing reviews conducted by accounting firms in connection with fund financial statement audits.

D. SEC Enforcement Actions Against Directors Regarding Valuation

The SEC has brought enforcement actions directly against directors, including independent directors, on several occasions over the past 20 years, which collectively provide some indication of how the SEC perceives directors' duties with respect to fair valuation.

In 2008, the SEC settled an enforcement action against the directors of two mutual funds managed by Heartland Advisors. The directors had approved pricing procedures that required the adviser's Pricing Committee to use a pricing service to fair value the funds' bonds in order to calculate NAV. The procedures also required the Pricing Committee to review the pricing service's valuations. During the time period covered by the action, the funds' portfolio managers became aware that projects underlying some of the bonds held by the funds were in default or were failing. The pricing service did not reduce the valuations based upon this information and the adviser continued to use these valuations without challenge. The pricing service gradually reduced the valuations of certain bonds incrementally, but not based upon any credit-related events affecting the bonds. The incremental price reductions had the effect of spreading out and minimizing the impact of valuation declines on the funds' NAV and performance. The adviser did not adjust the prices of the funds' securities despite numerous indications that the bonds could only be sold at substantial discounts to their marked values. Although the directors contended that the adviser had misled them regarding the status of the funds, and had hired experts to assist them in performing their duties, the SEC found that the directors were negligent in their failure to adequately monitor the liquidity of the funds and to take adequate steps to address the funds' pricing deficiencies. The SEC acknowledged that the directors had inquired about the pricing and liquidity issues that came to their attention, but the SEC alleged that the directors did not go far enough in following through and resolving those issues as required by their duties arising under the 1940 Act. In particular, the SEC alleged that the directors did not direct the Pricing Committee to stop using the pricing service's prices, even though they had received information suggesting that the service's prices were higher than the prices at which the funds could reasonably expect to sell the bonds.

In June 2013, the SEC settled an enforcement proceeding against eight former directors of investment companies (the Morgan Keegan funds) advised by Morgan Asset Management, Inc., finding that the directors (including the independent directors) caused the funds to violate Rule 38a-1 in not adopting policies and procedures reasonably designed to prevent violations of the federal securities laws concerning the fair value of portfolio securities. The initial enforcement proceeding had alleged that the directors failed to satisfy their statutory obligations under the federal securities laws to fair value the funds' portfolio securities. The SEC had alleged that the board did not know and did not inquire as to the manner in which the adviser's valuation committee and the fund accounting department made fair value determinations of particular types of securities and did not receive information that would allow the directors to understand the methodology that was being used to fair value securities. In a separate action against the adviser and the portfolio manager, among others, the SEC charged that the valuations of certain securities were stale and had been inappropriately influenced by the fund's portfolio manager.

Together, the *Heartland* and *Morgan Keegan* matters underscore the importance of director attention to, and vigilance during all stages of, the valuation process. The *Heartland* matter shows that directors should monitor methodologies used by third parties, such as the fund's adviser or a pricing service, for continued appropriateness and take action when the methodologies do not appear to be followed. In *Morgan Keegan*, the SEC's finding of a violation of Rule 38a-1 should remind directors to carefully consider the various aspects of valuation procedures—to consider who is making valuation decisions (and any conflicts they might have), to understand the methodologies used and to determine if the procedures are being followed and remain accurate, particularly in times of market dislocation or distress.

Compliance Programs

A. Required Policies and Procedures

Under the 1940 Act, each fund is required to adopt and implement written policies and procedures that are reasonably designed to prevent violations of the federal securities laws. The fund's board, including a majority of the independent directors, must approve these policies and procedures, as well as policies and procedures of each investment adviser (including sub-advisers), the principal underwriter, administrator, and transfer agent of the fund, after finding that the policies and procedures are reasonably designed to prevent violation of the federal securities laws by the fund and by each investment adviser, principal underwriter, administrator and transfer agent of the fund. Directors may satisfy their obligations by reviewing summaries of the compliance programs prepared by the fund's CCO or other persons familiar with the programs provided that such summaries familiarize the directors with the salient features of the programs. The SEC has stated that fund compliance policies and procedures should address, at a minimum, the pricing of the fund's portfolio securities, the processing of orders for its shares, the identification of affiliated persons, the protection of nonpublic information regarding the fund, adherence to fund governance requirements, and policies as to market timing. (See Section 7.A(3) for a discussion of the directors' general oversight responsibilities to monitor the risk management, internal control, and compliance practices of the investment adviser and others to whom responsibilities have been delegated.)

B. Role of the Chief Compliance Officer

Each fund must have a chief compliance officer, or CCO, who is responsible for administering the fund's compliance program. The CCO has been called the "eyes and ears" of the fund's independent directors, and as a matter of general practice many CCOs will attend all or a portion of every board meeting. The fund board, including a majority of the independent directors, must approve the appointment and compensation of the CCO, as well as any changes in the compensation. In reviewing the CCO's compensation, boards typically consider whether the amount of compensation is sufficient to retain qualified individuals in the role, and whether the structure of the compensation (e.g., base versus bonus components) leads to appropriate incentives for the CCO. At any time, the board may remove the CCO, who may not be terminated as the fund's CCO by the investment adviser or another service provider without the board's consent. The CCO may also be the CCO for the investment adviser and may be compensated in whole or in part by the adviser. This is not inappropriate and, in the release adopting the compliance rule (the "Adopting Release"), the SEC states that it expects that often the fund's CCO will be employed by the adviser and also be the adviser's CCO. Directors should be aware of both the potential benefits and the potential conflicts of interest that may arise from this arrangement.

The CCO is responsible for keeping the board apprised of significant compliance events at the fund and its service providers and for advising the board of needed changes in the fund's compliance program. The fund's CCO reports directly to the fund board and at least annually must furnish the board with a written report on the operation of the fund's policies and procedures and those of its service providers. The report must address, at a minimum: (i) the operation of the policies and procedures of the fund and each service provider since the last report, (ii) any material changes to the policies and procedures since the last report, (iii) any recommendations for material changes to the policies and procedures as a result of the annual review, and (iv) any material compliance matters since the date of the last report. While the rule requires annual reports to the board to discuss material compliance matters that occurred since the date of the last report, the Adopting Release notes that the reporting to the board of all such compliance matters cannot necessarily be delayed until the next annual report. The CCO must meet in executive session with the fund's independent directors at least once a year. Many boards meet more frequently with the CCO and some boards designate an independent director to serve as a liaison with the CCO between board meetings.

The SEC rule, Rule 38a-1, that established the compliance program and CCO requirements has been viewed in a mixed light by boards and the industry. The core goals of the rule are readily understood, and the establishment of the CCO position and formal compliance programs have been viewed as a positive development that enhances and focuses board oversight. The rule also—and more controversially—has been used by the SEC as an enforcement tool, with so-called "compliance program cases" brought against organizations, individual compliance officers, and even fund boards in connection with fund policies and procedures relating to a variety of issues, including valuation. The cases generally allege some combination of a lack of or poor compliance program design, laxity of implementation, ineffective oversight, and the like, and the rule has been applied in situations where underlying violations of federal securities laws have not been proven by the SEC.

C. Oversight of Service Providers

As noted above, the fund's board, including a majority of the independent directors, is required to approve the written compliance policies and procedures of the fund's principal investment adviser, its underwriter, its administrator, its transfer agent and any sub-advisers, insofar as they relate to the fund. The fund's CCO typically oversees the compliance programs of these service providers on behalf of the board. The CCO's written annual report must include an assessment of the operation of the compliance policies and procedures of the service providers.

As mutual fund platforms relying on sub-adviser and multi-manager strategies continue to become more common and to grow in scale, a challenge often faced by directors and fund CCOs is oversight of multiple sub-adviser compliance programs. As with all aspects of dealing with sub-advisers, there will be different approaches to addressing that challenge. But some level of systematization of compliance program reporting from the sub-advisers to the board and CCO will be important, as will due diligence before sub-advisers' compliance policies and procedures are presented to fund boards for approval.

D. CFTC Compliance

As to registered funds that operate as commodity pools, the CFTC has effectively harmonized most of its CPO rules, adopted pursuant to the CEA, on disclosure, reporting and recordkeeping, with those of the SEC. As a result, a CPO of a fund may elect to comply with most CFTC requirements through "substituted compliance" with applicable securities laws and SEC regulations. In order to utilize the substituted compliance approach, a fund's CPO must, among other things (1) file a notice with the NFA and (2) file with the NFA a fund's financial statements prepared in connection with its SEC reporting obligations. A CPO of a fund with less than a three-year operating history must also disclose the performance of all accounts and pools that are operated by the CPO with substantially similar investment objectives, policies and strategies. CPOs of funds that rely on substituted compliance nevertheless remain subject to examination and oversight by the CFTC and NFA, allowing CFTC enforcement actions to be brought for non-compliance with federal securities laws and for violations of the anti-fraud and anti-manipulation provisions of the CEA. The CFTC has also indicated that its harmonization rules are subject to future reconsideration. Fund directors should be satisfied that procedures are in place to ensure that the fund and its adviser comply with the CFTC's harmonization rules.

The SEC's Division of Investment Management has issued guidance for dually registered funds that rely on substituted compliance. The guidance reiterates that fund boards should oversee proper management of commodities interests and their associated risks, and that there is adequate disclosure to investors. As a best practice, directors should consider CFTC and NFA, as well as SEC, guidance directly applicable to derivatives-related compliance policies and procedures and disclosure to investors. The extent of the board's role in the risk oversight of the fund and the effect that it has on the board's leadership structure must also be included in a fund's statement of additional information. Directors of funds that are not commodity pools should exercise appropriate oversight to confirm there is a compliance program in place to monitor the continued applicability of the CFTC's exclusion from the definition of "commodity pool operator" (see Section 2.D). Directors should refer specific questions about CFTC and CEA compliance to legal counsel with specialization in this area.

Board Oversight of Use of Derivatives and Alternative Investment Strategies

A. Introduction

There are no technical legal definitions for the terms "derivatives" and "alternative investment strategies," and the investment management industry does not use them in a consistent manner. This section of the Guidebook attempts to generally describe derivatives and alternative investment strategies and their risks, explains the applicable regulatory framework, and provides suggestions for board oversight.

As a practical matter, the term "derivatives" commonly refers to futures contracts, forward contracts, options, swaps and other instruments whereby the value of the instrument is determined based upon, or derived from, that of another asset or reference (such as an interest rate or index level). Derivatives may involve operational and investment complexities relating to trading, settlement, valuation, liquidity, and accounting, and some derivatives entail implicit leverage, while others do not. Derivatives also may involve exposure to counterparties that should be monitored and managed.

The term "alternative investment strategy" generally connotes a non-traditional investment strategy. The SEC staff suggests that alternative investments include investments in hedge funds, private equity, venture capital, real estate and funds of private funds. That definition focuses on the structure of the product as well as the nature of the underlying investments. Alternative investment strategies include, for example, long/short strategies, managed futures, event arbitrage, and written options programs, which historically were offered only through institutional investment channels. Many alternative investment strategies are dependent on the use of derivatives, leverage and/or investments in illiquid and difficult to price securities.

A fund may use derivatives as part of its traditional investment strategies or its alternatives strategies. Particular investment strategies may call for the use of derivatives to hedge the exposures associated with other positions in the fund, or simply to obtain exposure to an asset class that is more cheaply acquired through the derivative than a physical position. For instance, currency forward contracts may be used to hedge the currency risks associated with investments in foreign securities or to obtain desired exposure to a foreign currency without ownership of an asset denominated in the currency. Futures contracts and swaps can be used to obtain investment exposure to certain securities or asset classes that may be otherwise costly and difficult to obtain. Some funds use derivatives to obtain leveraged exposure to an asset class, subject to requirements of the 1940 Act as interpreted by the SEC or the SEC staff (see Section 7.B(10)). For the reasons set forth below, fund use of derivatives generally deserves the attention of fund boards. Certain derivatives allow a fund to obtain investment exposure in excess of the amount of assets deployed, but the derivatives entail a risk of loss that is also greater than the amount of assets deployed. Under some circumstances, a fund's exposure as a result of a derivative may be difficult to quantify.

In addition to investment risks, the use of derivatives and many alternative investment strategies may entail other risks that boards should be aware of, and that management can identify and monitor. For instance, derivatives frequently require manual operational processes, including with respect to position confirmation, collateral movement, and order placement and settlement. While the overall need for manual processes is declining over time, derivatives still can entail operational risks for a fund. Order management systems must be able to communicate with fund accounting systems and be otherwise compatible. Many alternative strategies involve sophisticated models that require accurate inputs and monitoring. Derivatives and alternative investment strategies demand significant resources to deal with operational, tax, accounting, and legal issues. They can involve multiple parties and interfaces between different groups of people in working in different locations and often for different fund service providers.

B. Applicable Law

Fund directors should be generally aware of the federal securities, commodities and tax laws that apply to a fund's use of derivatives and alternative investment strategies, and obtain assurances that the fund's investment adviser has personnel and processes in place to ensure compliance with the applicable legal requirements. This section will provide directors with a working vocabulary about these requirements, and some ideas for the deployment of the fund CCO to address the associated compliance issues.

1) Public Disclosures

First and foremost, applicable law and regulations govern the content of disclosures to shareholders about the use of derivatives and the nature of alternative strategies. The SEC has stated that a fund's use of derivatives presents challenges for the fund's investment adviser and board to ensure that the derivatives are employed in a manner consistent with the fund's investment objectives, policies and restrictions, the fund's risk profile and relevant regulatory requirements. The fund's investment objectives, policies and restrictions are required to be disclosed in its registration statement, and the fund's investment portfolio must be consistent with that disclosure. Disclosures specific to derivative instruments typically describe the types of derivatives used, how the instruments work, whether derivatives are used for investment (including to increase exposure through effective leverage) or hedging purposes and key risks, including counterparty exposure, volatility of returns, valuation and liquidity. Fund boards should take steps to be satisfied that the fund's public disclosures accurately reflect the types of derivatives used by the fund, the extent of derivatives usage and applicable risks. Boards can do so by understanding the drafting process that is followed to help ensure that actual derivatives use is appropriately described in the public disclosures, including review by the investment professionals responsible for managing a fund's investments.

2) Other Applicable Securities Regulations

The use of derivatives and alternative investment strategies also implicates 1940 Act provisions regarding valuation, investment liquidity, diversification of fund holdings, concentration in particular industries, custody and restrictions on leverage. Funds using derivatives typically adopt policies and procedures relating to the leverage that can be obtained through the use of derivatives through asset segregation and the use of offsetting transactions (see Section 7.B(10)). Other fund policies and procedures that may be implicated by derivatives usage include those relating to valuation, liquidity, investment-related restrictions (e.g., diversification and concentration), and counterparty exposure. The SEC has acknowledged that there is some uncertainty regarding the application to some types of derivative transactions of the prohibitions and restrictions of the 1940 Act regarding senior securities and leverage (such as asset segregation requirements), investments in securities-related issuers, portfolio diversification and concentration, and valuation, among others, and indicated that additional guidance will be forthcoming. Boards can consider working with the fund CCO to assess fund compliance with those legal requirements, using a flexible approach that reflects the legal uncertainties in this area of the law and regulatory developments.

3) Tax Provisions and Cayman Subsidiaries

An additional issue can arise for funds that use derivative instruments to provide direct or indirect exposures to commodities. In order for a fund to offer its shareholders meaningful commodities exposures (for instance, more than 10% of the fund's income on an annual basis), the fund must establish a wholly-owned subsidiary to house those investments. Typically, a fund will establish the vehicle under the laws of the Cayman Islands, and will refer to it as a controlled foreign corporation ("CFC"). Under applicable tax law, the fund cannot invest more than 25% of its assets in that subsidiary. In most cases, the CFC will have its own board of directors, sometimes made up of personnel of the adviser or its affiliates, and sometimes including independent directors of the parent fund. The ability of a fund to use a CFC is largely conditioned on representations that the CFC will not be used to evade the requirements of the 1940 Act. A fund board should oversee the investment activities of the CFC by disregarding the structure, and viewing the assets of the CFC as if they were held directly by the fund.

If initial margins and premiums on the fund's non-hedging investments in futures, options on futures and certain swaps exceed 5% of the fund's assets or the notional value of such investments exceed 100%

of fund assets, the fund will not be eligible for an exemption from the CFTC's requirement that the fund's adviser be registered with the CFTC as a CPO. Boards should be satisfied that the fund's compliance policies and procedures address these matters (see Section 9.D).

C. Practical Guidance on Oversight

As a starting point, directors should understand any direct and indirect risks created or elevated by a fund's use of derivatives and how these risks are managed by the appropriate fund service providers. Federal law requires disclosures (including in the statement of additional information) regarding the board's role in the fund's risk management process. In addition to investment risks (including risks arising from exposure to the underlying assets or reference and counterparty exposure), boards should consider the need for enhanced valuation and liquidity oversight and compliance and operational services, as well as the operational risks of any fund service providers involved in derivatives transactions and related monitoring. Boards can work with the fund CCO to understand how areas of potential compliance uncertainty are addressed by the fund's service providers.

Directors should have a working understanding of the investment case for any derivatives or alternative investment strategy to be used by a fund, including an understanding of the degree to which a strategy depends on leverage and derivatives use. As a practical matter, fund boards take varied approaches to overseeing a fund's use of derivatives and engagement in alternative investment strategies. One size does not fit all. The approach of any board should be aligned with the degree to which the derivatives and alternative strategies put the fund's assets at the risk of loss. For example, a board that oversees funds that use derivatives only occasionally and in a limited way could reasonably take a different approach than a board that oversees a fund that uses derivatives extensively. Some boards receive periodic reports concerning a fund's use of derivatives and related compliance matters. Directors also can review fund financial statements to assess the degree to which a fund uses derivatives because financial reporting requirements call for clear disclosure to shareholders about derivative positions, their sizes, their general uses, and information about counterparties.

Some boards identify an individual within the adviser who understands the operational workings necessary to successfully use derivatives and request that he or she report to the directors on an ongoing basis. The goal is to seek to obtain enough information from the adviser to allow the board to assure itself that the adviser has the requisite investment expertise to use the instruments and adequate operational and risk processes in place to be able to use the derivatives or alternative investment strategy for the fund in an appropriate and anticipated way.

As with other risk oversight responsibilities, directors do not need to be experts in these areas. Rather, they should seek to be informed and speak up when they see red flags.

Disclosure Requirements

A. Disclosure Materials

The principal disclosure materials of a fund are (i) the registration statement and prospectus used in connection with the sale of shares, (ii) annual and semi-annual reports filed with the SEC and periodic reports sent to shareholders, and (iii) proxy statements used in connection with shareholder meetings. There are also special disclosure requirements related to certain distributions by funds and to proxy voting with respect to portfolio securities.

1) Registration Statements and Prospectuses

Mutual funds engaged in a continuous offering must register, on a continuous basis, the sale of their securities with the SEC. Directors have a federal statutory responsibility for the accuracy of a fund's registration statements filed with the SEC in connection with the fund's offering of the securities to the public. A director, whether or not he or she signs the registration statement, is personally liable for any material inaccuracy or omission in the registration statement, including information incorporated by reference from other filed documents, unless a defense is available.

The director's primary defense to registration statement liability is "due diligence." To establish that defense, the director must show that, after reasonable investigation, the director had reasonable grounds to believe, and did believe, that the registration statement did not contain any materially false or misleading statements or any material omissions that made the registration statement misleading. Actions required by the director to satisfy the due diligence standard will vary with the circumstances. Directors are well advised to satisfy themselves that, in preparing the registration statement, fund management follows procedures reasonably designed to ensure its accuracy and completeness. Directors would be wise to be familiar with the contents of the registration statement and prospectus, especially those areas that are within their knowledge and competence.

The U.S. Supreme Court's 2011 decision in *Janus Capital Group, Inc. v. First Derivative Traders* has prompted fund directors to reconsider their funds' potential liability, and the potential liability of the directors, for the content of fund prospectuses. While the *Janus* decision did not change registration statement liability for funds or their directors, many fund boards have been devoting more attention to reviewing the process by which registration statements of their funds are drafted, reviewed, and approved since the decision. In the *Janus* case, public shareholders of the investment adviser of the Janus funds sought to hold the adviser liable for allegedly misleading statements in the funds' prospectuses. The Court held that the adviser could not be held liable for the contents of the prospectuses, reasoning that only persons who actually "made" the statements could be liable for their contents, in this case, the funds themselves.

After *Janus*, many fund boards have reviewed and, in many cases, enhanced their practices for engaging in "due diligence" regarding the content of fund registration statements and other material communications to fund shareholders. For example, many boards request that the fund's adviser report to the board on its process for preparing the fund's materials, including how the fund's prospectus is prepared and vetted, and by whom; and whether persons familiar with the fund's investment program, including the portfolio manager, have reviewed and signed off on the investment strategy and risk disclosures. Some boards also have reconsidered provisions of the funds' advisory contract that discuss the adviser's responsibility for the accuracy of information included in the fund's registration statements and sought assurances from advisers regarding such information. Many boards also have reviewed their D&O/E&O insurance coverage with respect to claims relating to alleged misstatements in prospectuses and other communications to shareholders.

As discussed in Section 11.B below, funds are required to maintain disclosure controls and procedures.

2) Reports to the SEC and Shareholders

Funds must file annual and semi-annual reports with the SEC and provide annual and semi-annual reports to shareholders, which include specified financial and other information. Funds must also file their complete portfolio holdings schedule with the SEC on a quarterly basis. This schedule must be made publicly available. Funds may include a summary portfolio schedule in their semi-annual reports to shareholders rather than the complete schedule. As a general rule, directors are not personally liable for the accuracy of these reports. They should, however, be alert for any material inaccuracies or omissions in the fund procedures designed to prevent such problems. The shareholder report must also contain disclosure as to how the boards evaluate and approve advisory arrangements and fees. (See Section 5.C for a discussion of the *Northern Lights* enforcement action brought by the SEC against fund directors.)

In 2015, the SEC proposed new reporting requirements which, if adopted, would require funds (other than money market funds) to report on a monthly basis detailed information about their portfolios, including derivative usage, risk metrics related to debt securities, counterparty exposure, and securities lending transactions, among other things. The new monthly reports would replace the quarterly reports on portfolio holdings required under current regulations. Under the proposal, only the information reported for the third month of a fund's fiscal quarter would be made publicly available, and only 60 days after the end of the fiscal quarter. The proposed reporting requirements are part of the SEC's ongoing effort to strengthen its ability to identify and address risks of specific types of funds and of the asset management industry as a whole.

3) Proxy Statements

Funds generally must comply with the federal securities laws relating to proxy statements. Directors should review such statements to confirm that, based upon their knowledge, there are no material misstatements or omissions including with respect to information about themselves. Directors, even independent directors who were not directly involved in the preparation of a proxy statement, may be at risk if they fail to exercise appropriate care in connection with their oversight of disclosure documents. Proxy statements involving fund mergers are also prospectuses filed as part of a registration statement and involve corresponding liabilities.

4) Disclosure of Proxy Voting

A fund must disclose in its registration statement the policies and procedures it (or its investment adviser) uses to determine how to vote proxies relating to portfolio securities, including procedures used when a vote presents a conflict between the interests of fund shareholders and those of the fund's investment adviser, principal underwriter, or affiliated persons. A fund must file its complete proxy voting record annually with the SEC and must make the proxy voting record available to shareholders upon request. The directors should review these proxy voting policies and procedures, with the goal that the proxies are being voted in the best interests of fund shareholders and that conflicts are being appropriately dealt with.

B. Certification of the Accuracy of Reports Filed with the SEC

The Sarbanes-Oxley Act requires that periodic reports filed with the SEC be certified by the principal executive officer ("CEO") and principal financial officer ("CFO") of the fund. Among other things, these officers must certify that they have read the report in question and that all financial and other information disclosed is materially correct. The rules require the CEO and CFOs to make specified certifications as to their evaluation of the fund's disclosure controls and procedures and their disclosures to the auditors and the audit committee about the fund's internal control over financial reporting. They must also certify that information has been included in the periodic shareholder reports as to their evaluation of internal control and any changes in internal control. The certification requirement is intended to improve the quality of the disclosure that a company provides about its financial condition in its periodic reports to investors and is designed to ensure that CEOs and CFOs are personally involved in the review of reports.

Funds are required to maintain disclosure controls and procedures designed to ensure that the information required in SEC filings and shareholder reports is properly processed and reported on a timely basis. Management of a fund, under the supervision and with the participation of the CEO and CFO, are required within the ninety day period prior to the filing date of each report requiring certification to evaluate the effectiveness of the fund's disclosure controls and procedures and present in the report the conclusion of the CEO and CFO as to such effectiveness. Although the directors have no specific responsibilities in connection with the disclosure certification requirements, these requirements are core provisions of the Sarbanes-Oxley Act, and, as part of their general oversight responsibilities, directors should be knowledgeable as to the procedures established by the fund and its investment adviser for compliance with the certification requirements.

SECTION **12**

Money Market Funds

Money market funds ("MMFs") are open-end investment companies registered under the 1940 Act that invest in high quality, short-term money market instruments. They offer investors relative safety of principal; a high degree of liquidity; a wide range of shareholder services (including check writing) and maintenance of a stable net asset value (NAV) usually $1.00 per share. MMFs are not protected by federal deposit insurance, and there is no guarantee that MMFs will be able to maintain a stable NAV.

As a result of significant rule changes adopted in 2014, beginning in 2016, only MMFs with shareholders limited to natural persons, and all government MMFs, can maintain a stable $1.00 NAV. MMFs (other than government MMFs) that allow institutional shareholders must float their NAV calculated to the fourth decimal point.

The role of a money fund's board of directors is of paramount importance in ensuring compliance with the requirements of Rule 2a-7, the rule that governs MMFs. In light of recent regulatory reforms, the role of the board of directors of MMFs again will increase.

During the 2008–2009 global financial crisis, the short-term credit markets froze, contributing to large-scale redemptions from MMFs. A notable casualty of the market turmoil, was a MMF that "broke the buck," prompting further concerns about liquidity. In response to this crisis, the federal government intervened in an unprecedented manner. The financial crisis, its impact on a large number of MMFs, and the need for government intervention were the catalysts for the SEC to adopt sweeping new MMF reforms in 2010 and again in 2014. The reforms were hotly debated.

On February 23, 2010, the SEC adopted significant amendments to Rule 2a-7 designed to make MMFs more resilient, facilitate the orderly liquidation of an MMF that breaks the buck, and improve the SEC's oversight of MMFs. The amendments imposed more stringent conditions with respect to credit quality, diversification, liquidity, and maturity of MMF's and required greater transparency and portfolio stress testing. The amendments also provided additional board powers permitting the board to suspend redemptions and postpone payment of redemption proceeds if a fund will "break the buck" and if the fund will irrevocably liquidate.

On July 23, 2014, a divided SEC adopted rules that will require floating NAVs for institutional money market funds (other than government MMFs), give money market funds the discretion to impose liquidity fees and gates, and require fees to be imposed at a certain threshold unless the fund's board determines not to impose a fee. The 3-2 vote, which closes the latest tumultuous chapter of money market fund regulatory reform, will fundamentally change the way that most money market funds operate.

The floating NAV requirement, which was designed to reduce the "first mover" advantage of MMF shareholders, will not apply to retail money market funds and all government money market funds (whether or not they are institutional funds).

The 2014 reforms increase the responsibility of MMF boards. MMF boards will be authorized to impose gates (for up to 10 business days in any 90 calendar day period) and redemption fees (up to 2% when a fund's weekly liquidity falls below 30% of its total assets); but when weekly liquidity drops below 10%, the fund must impose a 1% redemption fee unless the directors determine that a lower fee, a higher fee, not to exceed 2%, or no fee at all would be in the best interests of the MMF's shareholders. Their actions, or inaction, likely will have a significant effect on investors and whether the MMF funds they oversee can continue to operate.

MMFs, investors, and regulators will wait to see whether the new rules achieve their stated goals.

The following is a summary of the responsibilities of directors under Rule 2a-7, certain of which may be delegated to the investment adviser.

A. Board Findings

For MMFs with a stable NAV, the board must determine in good faith that it is in the best interests of the fund and its shareholders to maintain a stable net asset value per share, by virtue of either the amortized cost method or the penny-rounding method. The MMF may continue to use that method only so long as the board of directors believes that it fairly reflects the market-based net asset value per share.

One of the most important requirements is that the MMF periodically "shadow price" the amortized cost of the fund's portfolio against the mark-to-market NAV of the portfolio. If there is a difference of more than one-half of 1%, the board must consider promptly what action, if any, should be taken, including whether the MMF should discontinue the use of the amortized cost method of valuation and re-price the securities of the MMF if the MMF breaks the buck, either below or above $1.00 per share.

B. Required Procedures

The board of an MMF that uses the amortized cost method of valuation must establish (and periodically review) written procedures reasonably designed to stabilize the fund's net asset value per share at $1.00. These procedures must provide for: (i) calculating the deviation of the fund's current net asset value per share from the amortized cost price per share at least daily and at such intervals as the board deems reasonable in light of market conditions; (ii) the periodic review by the board of the amount of the deviation and the methods used for its calculation; and (iii) prompt consideration by the board of what action, if any, should be initiated if the deviation from the fund's amortized cost price exceeds one-half of 1%. MMFs must adopt procedures with respect to using the penny-rounding method designed to ensure that the price per share, rounded to the nearest 1%, will not deviate from the single price established by the board of directors.

C. Oversight

The board must establish the MMF's procedures and oversees their implementation. It should review periodically the MMF's investments and the investment adviser's procedures in connection with investment decisions. The SEC, however, believes that the board, not the investment adviser, is the appropriate entity to determine when and how an MMF will impose liquidity fees and/or redemption gates, within the confines of the rule.

D. Valuation

As with all mutual funds, MMFs must value their portfolio securities at their current market value when market quotations are readily available. They must value securities for which no readily available market value exists at fair value as determined in good faith by the board of directors. The SEC acknowledges that the vast majority of MMF portfolio securities do not have readily available market quotations because most portfolio securities such as commercial paper, repurchase agreements, and certificates of deposit are not actively traded in the secondary markets. For this reason, MMF portfolio securities are valued largely upon "mark-to-model" or "matrix pricing" estimates.

The SEC has provided guidance to MMF directors as to the factors they should consider when using these fair value market methodologies. Similarly, the SEC has provided guidance to MMF directors who use a pricing service to assist them in determining fair values of portfolio securities. MMF directors should be familiar with their pricing responsibilities and the guidance that the SEC has provided in this regard (see Section 8).

E. Portfolio Quality

An MMF must limit its investments to those securities determined by its board to present minimal credit risk (which must include factors pertaining to credit quality in addition to securities ratings).

F. Security Downgrades

The board must act promptly if a portfolio security becomes ineligible for investment by the fund because of a decline in its credit quality. Directors must reassess whether the security presents minimal credit risk and must cause the fund to take such action as they determine to be in the fund's best interests. The board is relieved of this responsibility if the security is sold or matures within five business days of the adviser's becoming aware of the new rating and the board subsequently is advised of the adviser's actions.

G. Security Defaults and Other Events

If a portfolio security defaults, becomes ineligible for purchase, or no longer presents minimal credit risk, the fund must dispose of the security promptly, unless the board determines that to do so would not be in the fund's best interest. This determination may take into account, among other factors, market conditions that could affect the orderly disposition of the security.

H. Delegation of Duties

The board may not delegate its duties related to the initial determination to use the amortized cost or penny-rounding method and the adoption of the required written procedures. The board may not delegate its duties in the event of deviation between the amortized cost method and net asset value using market quotations resulting in material dilution or unfair results or if such deviation is in excess of one-half of 1%. The board also may not delegate certain of its responsibilities in the event of a security default or downgrade except in those instances where the adviser determines that disposal of the portfolio security in question would not be in the best interests of the fund. Other duties generally may be delegated to the MMF's investment adviser, provided that the board establishes guidelines, reviews them periodically, and otherwise exercises adequate oversight.

The duties of MMF directors with respect to liquidity requirements (see Section 7.B(10)) and investments in derivative securities (see Section 10) are heightened because of the special nature of MMFs.

Closed-end Funds

A. Overview

Duties of directors of closed-end funds are generally similar to those of open-end funds. However, there are some differences, which largely reflect a few principal factors.

1) Differences between Closed-end and Open-end Funds

Closed-end funds, unlike open-end funds, do not stand ready to redeem their shares daily at net asset value, nor do they normally engage in continuous public offerings of their shares. As a result, closed-end funds do not need the liquidity of investments or cash reserves maintained by open-end funds to meet redemption demands. Like other corporations, closed-end funds can raise capital through public or private borrowings, or offerings of preferred or common stock. Requirements under the 1940 Act specifically applicable to closed-end funds recognize these differences by providing greater flexibility for leverage than is available to open-end funds and by permitting rights offerings for common shares of closed-end funds when they are trading at a discount to their net asset value. Closed-end funds, like open-end funds, may invest in almost any type of asset and pursue a wide variety of investment strategies.

Because closed-end funds do not need to stand ready to redeem their portfolios on a daily basis, closed-end funds generally are not limited by the SEC, as are open-end funds, in the percentage of their portfolios that may be invested in illiquid securities.

2) Regulation of Closed-end Funds

Liquidity to shareholders of closed-end funds generally is provided through listing and open-market trading on stock exchanges. Thus closed-end funds are regulated under the 1934 Act and applicable stock exchange requirements, including those relating to the composition, duties and powers of audit committees, and related disclosure in proxy statements. As publicly traded companies, closed-end funds are also subject to SEC requirements regulating selective disclosure of information, and their directors are subject to 1934 Act regulation of insider trading.

3) Shareholder Meetings

Listed closed-end funds, unlike many open-end funds, are required by stock exchange regulations to hold annual meetings of shareholders. These annual meetings provide regular forums for proposals and board nominations by shareholders. Although proxy-soliciting rules under the 1934 Act are applicable to shareholder solicitations by both open-end and closed-end funds, the requirement that closed-end funds hold annual meetings of shareholders makes these rules of much greater practical significance to closed-end funds. (See Section 4.A(2) for information as to the extent to which open-end funds must have shareholder meetings.)

4) Tendency of Closed-end Fund Shares to Trade at a Discount

The market prices of closed-end fund shares, like those of other publicly traded companies, are subject to the forces of supply and demand. Although shares of closed-end funds sometimes trade at premiums to their net asset value, they frequently trade at discounts from net asset value. The tendency of shares of closed-end funds to trade at discounts has resulted in significant shareholder activism, often presenting issues for consideration by their boards of directors (see Section 13.H).

B. Senior Securities and Leverage

Unlike open-end funds, closed-end funds are permitted, within limits imposed by the 1940 Act, their organizational documents and their investment policies, to issue debt securities and preferred stock (referred to in Section 18 of the 1940 Act as types of "senior securities") in addition to common equity securities. Since the 1940 Act's asset coverage requirements are more lenient for preferred stock than debt, closed-end funds may obtain significantly more leverage through the issuance of preferred stock than the issuance of debt or through bank borrowings. Directors are responsible for determining the appropriateness of issuing senior securities, based in part on the amount outstanding. Directors should understand the risks, costs and benefits of leverage and should monitor their fund's use of leverage to oversee that management uses leverage in an appropriate and prudent manner.

Closed-end funds have several options for obtaining leverage, including bank borrowings, often pursuant to a credit agreement provided by a syndicate of banks, entering into reverse repurchase agreements, issuance of fixed or variable rate preferred stock or margin facilities. As discussed in Section 10, they may also obtain effective leverage through the use of derivatives. Closed-end municipal funds often utilize tender option bonds or preferred stock, as their options are limited due to federal income tax considerations.

Historically many closed-end funds issued auction-rate preferred stock ("ARPS"). During the 2008–2009 financial crisis, the market for ARPS "froze" due to failed auctions, the result of more sellers than buyers for the ARPS, and the outstanding ARPS began to pay preferred dividends at default rates. While many closed-end funds eventually redeemed their outstanding ARPS at liquidation preference (sometimes referred to as "at par") in accordance with their terms, others have chosen to only partially redeem the ARPS, conduct tender offers for ARPS at less than liquidation preference, or have left them outstanding.

Plain vanilla preferred stock may also be used by closed-end funds to add leverage. The 1940 Act provides various rights to preferred stock holders, including separate approval rights with respect to a proposed plan of reorganization or investment policy changes that require shareholder approval. Preferred shareholders also must have the right, as a class, to elect at least two directors at all times and to elect a majority of directors if the fund does not pay dividends to the preferred share-holders for a period of two years. The duties of directors elected by the preferred shareholders are the same as the duties of a closed-end fund's other directors under the laws of most states, including Maryland, Delaware, and Massachusetts.

C. Offerings of Common Equity

Closed-end fund initial public offerings are typically underwritten public offerings organized by a syndicate of underwriters led by a group of lead managers. Some closed-end funds make subsequent underwritten offerings of their shares, and some make offerings into the market from time to time. Since fund shares may normally not be offered at prices of less than NAV, and since many closed-end funds tend to trade at a discount to net asset value, such offerings may be challenging to execute except when high demand for a fund's shares results in the shares trading above or close to NAV for a sustained period. Any public offering of a closed-end fund's shares must be made pursuant to an effective registration statement, and directors should be satisfied that all relevant requirements have been met in connection with any such offerings. They should also be sure that the costs of offerings, which can be considerable, are quantified by a manager and taken into account by the board in reaching a judgment as to whether any offering of a fund's shares is in the best interests of the fund. Directors should have a good understanding of the complete economics of a proposed transaction. These may involve payments of structuring, distribution, and other fees by the fund's investment manager or one of its affiliates, payment of sales charges by investors participating in the offering, and payments of organizational (in the case of the initial public offering) and offering expenses by the fund itself. As in the case of rights offerings, directors must also take account of the fact that fund managers, underwriters, distribution consultants and other service providers have a conflict of interest in recommending offerings of shares by a fund since successful sales of shares will result in increased compensation to such persons.

Offerings of fund shares can raise independence issues for directors if they are "interested persons" of a "principal underwriter" of the fund. A "principal underwriter" includes any underwriter that is a party to a distribution agreement with the fund. Thus, for example, each lead manager and each member of an underwriting syndicate for an offering by a fund is a "principal underwriter" of the fund for the time of the offering and, in some cases, a longer period. In some cases, independent directors may be asked to sell any securities they own that are issued by public companies that control a dealer-manager for a rights offering or a syndicate member for an underwritten public offering to deal with this issue.

Closed-end funds, unlike open-end funds, are not subject to the prohibition on using fund assets to pay for distribution expenses except pursuant to a Rule 12b-1 plan. Some closed-end funds, particularly continuously offered funds, have elected to make payments for ongoing shareholder servicing or investor relations, while others have obtained exemptive orders to permit the issuance of multiple classes of shares and to impose asset-based distribution fees and early withdrawal charges.

After the fund's initial public offering, some closed-end funds raise additional capital through the offering of common shares, generally through offerings of transferable or nontransferable rights. Section 23(b) of the 1940 Act prohibits closed-end funds from selling their common shares at below their net asset value except under limited circumstances. The exception usually relied upon is that permitting a rights offering to existing shareholders. The SEC requires the directors of closed-end funds to make a good faith determination that a rights offering will result in a net benefit to existing shareholders. This means that the directors must determine that the benefits of the rights offering to both subscribing and nonsubscribing shareholders outweigh the resulting dilution of per share net asset value and other negative effects. Benefits may include, for example, the anticipated return on investment of the proceeds, a reduction in per share expense ratio and the opportunity for shareholders to purchase shares at below net asset value. Dilution will result both from the sale of shares at below net asset value and the costs of conducting the offering, including any dealer-manager fees. Other negative effects may include a potential adverse impact on the short-term or long-term market prices of the fund's shares resulting from the market overhang or increased trading float during and after consummation of the rights offering. The offering of transferable rights gives nonsubscribing shareholders the opportunity to offset in part the dilutive effect of the rights offering through sale of their rights in the open market.

Although they may rely on information provided by the fund's investment manager and any proposed dealer-manager for the rights offering, independent directors should understand that each has an inherent conflict of interest resulting from the prospect either of increased advisory fees or dealer-manager fees earned as a result of the offering. They should also be mindful that transaction costs of the offering can be significant, especially if the fund pays solicitation fees to a dealer, which may be an affiliate of the fund's adviser, for encouraging shareholders to participate. Independent directors, therefore, should consult with independent counsel in connection with their determination of whether a rights offering is likely to result in a net benefit to shareholders and consider carefully whether they have sufficient information to make that decision.

D. Illiquid Investments

The SEC limits investment by open-end funds in illiquid securities to 15% of net assets. This limitation reflects concerns relating to the need of open-end funds to maintain liquidity to meet redemptions. As closed-end funds do not have these ongoing pressures for liquidity, there is no such general limitation on closed-end funds. Substantial investment in illiquid securities by closed-end funds can, however, affect liquidity for portfolio management and other corporate purposes and the complexity of portfolio valuation for any applicable asset coverage tests, the calculation of advisory fees and the publication of net asset value. While the 1940 Act requires closed-end funds to report their net asset values semi-annually, most closed-end funds report on a daily or weekly basis. Directors should understand and actively monitor their fund's policies and practices with regard to investment in illiquid securities.

Directors should also carefully review the adequacy of their fund's valuation policies and procedures. Closed-end funds must comply with the requirements of the 1940 Act, including the requirement to price portfolio securities for which market quotations are not readily available at fair value as determined in good faith by the board of directors. Illiquid assets are more likely to fall into the fair value category (see Section 8).

Although they have much greater flexibility to invest in illiquid securities than open-end funds, many closed-end funds invest primarily or exclusively in liquid securities such as publicly traded equities and preferred stock or high yield bonds, municipal bonds, convertible bonds, foreign securities, or leveraged loans for which a liquid market exists. In recent years the market has seen a proliferation of leveraged loan funds. Leveraged loans, which are senior secured floating rate loans made by banks to corporations, currently represent a large, liquid asset class that historically has experienced a lower correlation with traditional asset classes. However, as leveraged loans are private contracts rather than negotiable securities, the time required to settle trades is longer, stretching out a month or more for some loans.

E. Interval Funds

An interval fund is a hybrid closed-end fund that has elected, pursuant to Rule 23c-3 under the 1940 Act, to repurchase a stated percentage (5–25%) of its outstanding common shares at net asset value at periodic intervals, e.g., quarterly, semi-annually or annually, subject to a repurchase fee not exceeding 2%. Because of the ongoing obligation to repurchase their shares, regulation of leverage and liquidity of interval funds under the 1940 Act is more stringent than for other closed-end funds. The terms of any debt securities or borrowings must provide flexibility for repayment, without premium or penalty, prior to each repurchase pricing date as needed to ensure compliance with the asset coverage requirements of Section 18 of the 1940 Act. In addition, an interval fund's board of directors must adopt written procedures designed to ensure that the fund has sufficient liquid assets to meet its periodic repurchase obligations.

Although Rule 23c-3 was adopted in 1993, few closed-end funds have relied on it to make periodic or discretionary repurchase offers. Directors should understand and carefully evaluate the costs and benefits of such repurchases before undertaking such a course, which requires the adoption of a fundamental policy that can be changed only with shareholder approval.

F. Share Repurchases

Closed-end funds, other than interval funds, are not required to repurchase their shares unless they have undertaken to do so in connection with their initial public offering or otherwise. When shares of a closed-end fund are trading at significant discounts from their net asset value, however, boards of directors frequently have determined that share repurchases are in the best interests of the fund. Purchases at below net asset value, for example, have an antidilutive benefit to a fund by increasing the fund's per share net asset value. Share repurchases are often made through open-market purchase programs. Sometimes they are made through tender offers at net asset value or at prices representing smaller discounts from net asset value than those available in the market.

Regulation of share repurchases under the 1940 Act is designed to ensure equal treatment of shareholders. Section 23(c) of the 1940 Act permits a closed-end fund to make open-market purchases of its shares, provided that the fund has informed shareholders within the preceding six months of its intent to make such purchases, and to make tender offers to shareholders (provided the same terms are applicable to all shareholders). In-kind tender offers for fund shares raise issues under Section 17 of the 1940 Act, which generally prohibits principal transactions with affiliated persons, unless SEC exemptive relief has been obtained. Directors reviewing proposals for in-kind tender offers may also be concerned about the likelihood of participation by retail shareholders, particularly if the closed-end fund holds securities that may be difficult for a retail investor to hold, such as international securities that are not listed in the United States.

Open-market repurchases by a listed closed-end fund are normally made in a manner that satisfies the safe harbor under 1934 Act Rule 10b-18 to avoid potential market manipulation liability under federal securities laws. Because the safe harbor imposes volume limitations based on the issuer's average trading volume, closed-end funds that are thinly traded (*e.g.*, because they are small in size or because the "float" that is available for trading is relatively small) may be severely limited in their ability to make open-market purchases of shares.

Privately negotiated repurchases by closed-end funds are regulated by the 1940 Act. Section 23(c) and Rule 23c-1 thereunder include a prohibition against repurchases from affiliated persons of a fund, e.g., 5% shareholders, and a requirement that the purchase price not be higher than market value or net asset value, whichever is lower.

G. SEC and Stock Exchange Regulation

The 1934 Act, the New York Stock Exchange and NASDAQ regulate the composition, duties and powers of audit committees of closed-end funds and related proxy statement disclosure. As publicly traded companies, closed-end funds are also subject to SEC Regulation FD, which generally prohibits selective disclosure of material information. Directors and officers of closed-end funds are subject to the requirements of the 1934 Act regulating insider trading.

1) Audit Committee Requirements

The New York Stock Exchange and NASDAQ require the boards of directors of listed companies, including closed-end funds, to appoint audit committees consisting of at least three members who are both independent, as defined, and "financially literate," as interpreted by the board in its business judgment, while at least one member must have accounting or related financial management expertise. Members of audit committees should have a sufficient understanding of fundamental financial reporting and internal control principles to understand and consider material financial reporting and internal control issues. In addition, the stock exchanges require boards of directors of listed companies to adopt audit committee charters setting forth the purpose, duties and annual performance evaluation of the committee. It is common for these charters to be reviewed on an annual basis. New York Stock Exchange rules require the audit committee of a closed-end fund to review and discuss the fund's annual audited financial statements and semi-annual financial statements, including the "Management's Discussion of Fund Performance," if one has been provided to shareholders.

Closed-end funds listed on the New York Stock Exchange must also disclose an audit committee member's simultaneous service on more than three audit committees (the so-called "three audit committee" rule), in addition to determining that such simultaneous service would not impair the ability of that member to effectively serve on the fund's audit committee. For purposes of this requirement, a director's service on multiple boards in the same fund complex is counted as service on one audit committee. The NASDAQ listing requirements do not address service on multiple audit committees. The compensation, duties and powers of audit committees of closed-end funds, including the need to disclose whether at least one member is an "audit committee financial expert," as defined by the SEC, are more fully described in Section 4.B(1).

Federal proxy rules require disclosure in a closed-end fund's proxy statement for its annual meeting of shareholders of the deliberations and composition of its audit committee. These rules also require inclusion in the proxy statement of a report of the audit committee stating, among other things, whether it has recommended to the board of directors the inclusion of the fund's audited financial statements in the fund's annual report to shareholders. SEC rules acknowledge that in making this recommendation, the audit committee can rely on the representations of management and the fund's auditors.

These 1934 Act and listing requirements impose obligations on the board of directors and the audit committee of a closed-end fund in addition to their general duties under state law. The board of directors and audit committee of a closed-end fund should consult with counsel at least annually as to the contents of the fund's audit committee charter and related disclosure in the fund's proxy statement.

2) Short-swing Profits

Section 16(a) of the 1934 Act requires, among other things, that directors of a publicly traded company file with the SEC reports as to their ownership of the company's equity securities. Section 16(b) provides generally that "short-swing" profits (i.e., profits on any purchase and sale, or sale and purchase, of the company's securities within six months) realized by the company's directors are recoverable by the company. Under Section 16 of the 1934 Act and Section 30(h) of the 1940 Act, directors and other insiders of a closed-end fund are required to disclose, in accordance with applicable SEC filing requirements, their holdings of, and transactions in, all securities of the fund (other than short-term paper) beneficially owned by them. A director's failure to make these filings on a timely basis must be publicly disclosed in the fund's proxy statement for its annual meeting of shareholders. The reporting deadline for trades by directors is two business days after the trade date. Because of the complexity of the rules under Section 16 and the potential penalties for non-compliance, close consultation by directors with counsel is recommended.

3) Insider Trading

Directors of closed-end funds, like directors of other publicly traded companies, are prohibited from (i) purchasing or selling securities when they possess material, nonpublic information about the fund,

(ii) "tipping" or disclosing such information to others who may use it in trading or (iii) giving others recommendations to buy or sell while in possession of such information. Information is material if there is a substantial likelihood that a reasonable investor would consider it important in deciding whether to buy, sell, or hold a security. Some believe that information may be considered material if, upon disclosure, it would likely affect the stock price. If there is any doubt whether information is material, legal guidance should be sought or, as a practical alternative, the information should be treated as material. Closed-end fund directors may become privy to nonpublic information, which may be material, such as information pertaining to a prospective tender offer or rights offering by the fund, a change in the fund's historical dividend rate or the impact on the fund of the bankruptcy of the issuer of one of its significant portfolio holdings.

Purchasing or selling by a director of a closed-end fund of a security based upon material, nonpublic information about the fund or merely passing the information on to someone else who acts on that information is illegal. Insider trading by a director may result in criminal prosecution, disgorgement of profits, fines and other sanctions in actions instituted by the SEC. Consequently, directors should exercise caution in their own trading activities and in discussing with others the information they learn in the course of performing their duties. Similarly, directors should exercise caution so that information learned through their service as officers or directors of other public companies is not improperly communicated to the fund and its affiliates.

H. Corporate Governance and the Discount

The tendency of closed-end fund shares to trade at a discount has resulted in shareholder activism seeking to cause boards of directors of closed-end funds to take action to reduce or eliminate the discounts. Actions proposed by shareholders have included open-ending, share repurchase programs, and liquidation. Shareholder proposals urging boards of directors to take actions to address a fund's discount are not uncommon, and proxy contests to replace incumbent directors have also been waged. Directors should understand the extent of their duties in this regard under both state corporate law and the federal proxy rules.

1) Duties and Powers of Directors

The SEC requires prominent disclosure in prospectuses for offerings of closed-end fund shares of the tendency of closed-end fund shares to trade at a discount from their net asset value. In addition, some underwriters have required closed-end funds to adopt various policies, which may be embodied in charter provisions, to address investors' concerns about the discount. These have included undertakings to consider discretionary actions, such as open-market share repurchases or tender offers, and mandatory actions, such as obligations to make tender offers or put an open-ending proposal to a vote of shareholders if shares trade for specified periods at stated discount levels (see Section 13.H(2)).

The SEC staff has expressed concern with inadequate or possibly misleading disclosure in fund prospectuses and other materials about possible steps, such as repurchases, to minimize the discount. The SEC has emphasized that, if closed-end funds indicate in the prospectus or other communications that they will take action to address the discount, any material conditions or qualifications to the actions must be clearly disclosed. The SEC staff will pay particular attention to the clarity or prominence of disclosure regarding corporate actions that address the discount, as well as whether actions ultimately taken by closed-end funds are consistent with the disclosure. For this reason, directors should oversee, and may want to confirm with counsel, that the fund's prospectus and other written communications accurately describe the fund's policy, if any, for addressing the discount.

The market value of a corporation's common stock is of obvious importance to shareholders and a legitimate concern of the board of directors. It is proper for directors of a closed-end fund to consider the benefits and costs to the fund of addressing the discount and to take action reasonably believed by them to be in the best interests of the fund. Directors' duties to direct the management of the business and affairs of the fund do not, however, necessarily include any obligation to deal with the market price of a fund's common shares. Directors acting within applicable standards of conduct under state law do not ordinarily breach their duties in failing to take action to address the discount. Directors of a closed-end fund may, however, have duties in this regard imposed as a result of obligations undertaken by the fund in connection with its initial public offering or otherwise.

Shareholders do not have the right under general principles of corporate law to take direct corporate action relating to the business and affairs of a corporation but must act through the board of directors. The oversight responsibility of the directors is designed to ensure that management is carried out in the interests of the fund and not the variable and conflicting interests of a changing shareholder base. For this reason, shareholder proposals to address the discount, such as proposals for open-ending or liquidation, typically must be cast as recommendations to the board of directors to take the specified actions. Although directors should give careful consideration to any advisory shareholder proposal approved by shareholders, their duty to direct the management of the business and affairs of the fund in the overall interests of the fund remains paramount. The recourse of shareholders dissatisfied with the governance of directors is to replace those directors through the proxy process.

Section 15(a)(3) of the 1940 Act, as interpreted by the SEC, provides shareholders the direct right to terminate investment advisory contracts. Some shareholders have proposed termination of advisory contracts, an action that would not directly affect the discount from net asset value at which shares of closed-end funds trade, to gain leverage to force boards of directors to take action to address the discount. Thus, events that require a fund to seek shareholder approval of the advisory contract (such as a change in control of the adviser), may give dissidents an opportunity to assert this leverage.

2) Actions to Address the Discount

Boards of directors of a closed-end fund may choose to take action to address discount levels at which shares of the fund are trading if they reasonably believe that they are acting in the best interests of the fund. Actions taken by boards of directors of closed-end funds include measures ranging from share repurchases to open-ending. Some funds' governing documents contain specific requirements for board consideration of actions if a significant discount persists for a specified time period.

Share repurchases can be effected through open-market purchases or tender offers for a limited percentage of a fund's outstanding shares either at net asset value or at a discount thereto. These repurchases are a particularly important area of regulation for closed-end funds and are subject to the rules under the 1934 Act and the relevant exchange. Although share repurchases may have a temporary favorable impact on discount levels, there is no evidence demonstrating that they have any long-term effect. There may, however, be other benefits to the fund, such as the antidilutive benefit of repurchasing shares at prices below net asset value.

Open-ending, by conversion or by merger into an open-end fund, is the only measure that permits continued operations while definitively eliminating the discount. Open-ending, however, is a fundamental change in structure with major effects that must be carefully considered by boards of directors. The major consequences of open-ending have been immediate, massive redemptions of shares, frequently of more than 50% of outstanding shares, and the need for the capability to distribute fund shares continuously to offset both immediate and ongoing redemptions. If the fund has issued preferred shares, the board must consider that in an open-end structure, the fund will not be allowed to have preferred shares outstanding. Another important consideration is whether the existing portfolio holdings of the fund will comply with the portfolio liquidity standards applicable to open-end funds, especially in the wake of large-scale redemptions. Tax consequences and increased per-share operating expenses must also be considered. Some of these consequences may be ameliorated if open-ending is accomplished through merger into an open-end fund with similar investment objectives.

Other measures to address the discount include the election of interval fund status and the adoption of a managed distribution policy. A closed-end fund that wishes to pursue interval fund status must adopt a fundamental policy, approved by a majority of the fund's outstanding voting securities, setting forth, among other things, the periodic intervals at which repurchases or distributions will be made. A managed distribution policy attempts to increase market demand for a closed-end fund's shares through the establishment of an attractive monthly, quarterly or other periodic distribution rate, e.g., 10% per annum, regardless of actual investment income or realized gains. If earnings are insufficient, a portion of distributions will consist of a return of capital. The implementation of a managed distribution policy normally will require a fund to obtain an exemptive order from the SEC due to the prohibition in Section 19(b) of the 1940 Act against making distributions of long-term capital gains more than once every 12 months with some limited exceptions.

In addition, or as alternatives, to the techniques discussed above, some funds engage firms to provide secondary market support, including public relations activities such as advertising and presenting at or sponsoring conferences attended by investment advisers, in hopes of moderating the discount. Some funds have merged in hopes of achieving operational economies or improving performance. Other funds have explored options including the addition of leverage (including borrowing) or liquidation. Each of the measures to address the discount has advantages and disadvantages, which must be considered in light of each fund's particular circumstances and applicable legal and regulatory requirements. Boards of directors of closed-end funds should consult with counsel, their fund's investment manager and other appropriate advisers before taking action to address the discount, to ensure that any action taken is a reasonable use of fund assets and in the best interests of the fund. Directors should be on guard for potential conflicts, and be aware that dissidents in such situations frequently allege that the directors and the adviser are seeking only to preserve their own positions and fees.

Notwithstanding any action the board may take, shareholders of a closed-end fund may seek to introduce shareholder proposals relating to the discount at the closed-end fund's annual or special meeting of shareholders. Inclusion of such a proposal in a proxy statement is subject to the proxy rules under the 1934 Act and the provisions of the fund's charter and by-laws. Subject to SEC rules, fund management may exclude such a shareholder proposal if shareholders do not have the power to require its inclusion under the laws of the fund's state of organization. Directors should have working familiarity with those state laws, or consult with counsel, in order to evaluate the potential impact of shareholder proposals.

3) Board Governance Measures

Directors may elect to adopt various measures designed to enhance and protect their power to direct the oversight of their fund in accordance with the allocation of power under state law between directors and shareholders. These measures may include: (i) establishing a classified board, *i.e.*, a board with staggered terms; (ii) adopting an advance notice bylaw requiring minimum advance notice of shareholder proposals or board nominations; (iii) establishing qualification requirements for nominees for election as directors (e.g., experience relevant to the fund's investment objective); (iv) requiring the approval of the holders of a majority of outstanding shares for the election of directors; (v) vesting exclusive power to amend bylaws in the board of directors; and (vi) adopting a shareholder rights plan. It is common in connection with the organization of a new closed-end fund to include charter provisions requiring a supermajority vote to effect extraordinary actions, such as open-ending, liquidation, or merger. The availability of these and other measures will depend upon applicable state law, and implementation of certain measures after a fund's initial public offering may require a vote of shareholders. However, the SEC staff has taken the position that Section 18(i) of the 1940 Act generally requires that every share issued by a fund be a voting share with equal voting rights, even if in conflict with state law, effectively eliminating the availability of certain anti-takeover tactics that restrict voting rights of large stockholders. In their deliberations concerning the adoption and implementation of these provisions, directors must adhere to state law standards of conduct and have a reasonable belief that they are acting in the best interests of the fund. Actions taken in the face of actual or threatened shareholder action may be subject to heightened scrutiny by the courts. Boards that adopt governance measures should fully disclose to shareholders their actions and implications.

4) *Federal Proxy Rules*

Stock exchange listing requirements impose an obligation on closed-end funds to hold annual meetings of shareholders even when not required under applicable state law. Shareholders are therefore able to make proposals or nominate directors each year. Federal law requires publicly owned companies, including investment companies, that solicit proxies for shareholder votes on election of directors or other matters to furnish each shareholder with a proxy statement, which must be filed with, and may be reviewed by, the SEC. Shareholders may file their own proxy statements to solicit proxies for their proposals and must do so to solicit proxies for their nominees for the board of directors. Shareholders frequently opt, however, to take advantage of Rule 14a-8 of the federal proxy rules, which permits timely proposals by qualified shareholders (but not director nominations) to be included in a fund's proxy statement for its annual meeting of shareholders. The rule also provides various grounds on which shareholder proposals may be excluded from the fund's proxy statement. To exclude a proposal, a company must first notify the SEC, which is typically done through a request for a "no-action" letter. The SEC has promulgated various FAQs in its implementation of Rule 14a-8 specifying the general types of shareholder proposals that would satisfy the Rule. Federal proxy rules also require a fund to disclose whether the nominating committee will consider nominations of directors by shareholders and the process for shareholder submissions of recommendations for director candidates.

Directors should review a proxy statement before it is filed with the SEC or disseminated to shareholders, to oversee that, based upon their knowledge, there are no material misstatements or omissions particularly with respect to information about themselves. This is particularly the case if non-routine matters or shareholder proposals are included. Directors also should determine the fund's position with respect to shareholder proposals or board nominees. It is proper for directors to authorize a fund to incur costs to oppose shareholder proposals or nominees for the board of directors if they reasonably believe they are acting in the best interests of the fund.

Some activists who have won board seats or had proposals approved have sought to obtain reimbursement for their proxy solicitation expenses. Proposed reimbursements of this type may need to be reviewed to ensure they do not run afoul of the 1940 Act's prohibition on joint transactions by a fund and an affiliated person.

Exchange-traded Funds

A. Overview

Exchange-traded funds ("ETFs") are hybrid investment companies that often are structured as open-end funds, but whose shares trade on securities exchanges in a manner similar to shares of listed closed-end funds. ETFs, similar to traditional open-end funds, may be classified as index-based or actively managed. An index ETF seeks to track the performance of a designated index either by holding all of the securities in the index in the same proportion as the index (commonly referred to as "replication") or by using a sampling or optimization technique, whereby the ETF's investment adviser selects a representative sample of the securities in the index to be held by the ETF. An active ETF does not seek to track the performance of a designated index. Instead, an active ETF's investment adviser manages the ETF's investments according to its investment objectives and policies, and often seeks to outperform its benchmark. Certain ETFs that are not open-end funds, such as trusts that hold physical commodities or essentially pursue their investment objective through use of futures contracts and related options, are not subject to the 1940 Act and are beyond the scope of this Guidebook.

The demand for ETFs continues to grow, driven by both institutional and retail investors. In general, index ETFs often offer investors the diversification benefits and relatively low expenses associated with index investing. In addition, all ETFs provide the ability for intraday trading and short selling, may provide certain tax efficiencies and have lower transfer agency and distribution expenses than conventional open-end funds.

B. Regulatory Framework

ETFs are subject to the same regulations as traditional open-end funds, and must comply with registration statement and diversification requirements, limits on leverage and liquidity, and requirements to calculate daily NAVs. However, due to the structure of ETFs, at this time ETFs must seek from the SEC exemptive relief from certain provisions of the 1940 Act and the rules thereunder in order to form and operate. Pursuant to the requirements of such exemptive relief, ETFs generally: disseminate their portfolio holdings daily, as opposed to only quarterly like traditional open-end funds; disclose the intraday indicative value of their portfolio; publish trading information about their shares, including the premiums and discounts at which their shares have historically traded; and list their shares on a national securities exchange. The SEC recently granted exemptive relief to permit the launch and operation of a new type of pooled investment vehicle known as an "exchange-traded managed fund" (ETMF). The ETMF will include certain features of ETFs, but will not provide the daily transparency currently required for actively managed ETFs. Other ETF sponsors are seeking relief from the SEC to offer active ETFs for which they will not disclose the daily portfolio holdings. Accordingly, the requirements applicable to different types of ETFs may change over time.

ETFs also may be subject to certain requirements of the exchanges on which they are listed, including, for example, heightened financial literacy requirements for audit committee members. However, unlike closed-end funds, ETFs often are exempted from certain listing requirements, such as holding annual shareholder meetings.

C. Purchasing and Redeeming Shares

Unlike traditional open-end funds, ETFs do not sell or redeem individual ETF shares at NAV. Instead, ETFs sell and redeem shares at NAV only in large blocks (generally comprised of at least 25,000 shares) referred to as "creation units." Creation units are issued to and redeemed from third parties called "authorized participants" or "APs," typically market makers, specialists or large institutional investors, each of whom has entered into an agreement with the ETF to act as an AP. The creation units are then broken into individual ETF shares by the AP and held or sold in the secondary market. Retail investors transact in individual ETF shares in the secondary market at prices that may be lower or higher than NAV.

ETFs generally issue and redeem creation units in-kind, although certain ETFs may issue and redeem creation units for cash or partially in-kind, depending on the nature of the ETF's portfolio holdings. For in-kind purchases and redemptions, ETFs publish daily "baskets" that set forth the names and quantities of securities and other assets that the ETFs will accept for a creation unit of shares and pay out in a redemption of a creation unit. In the creation, an AP provides the securities and other assets comprising the basket in return for the creation unit of shares; and in a redemption, an AP receives the securities and other assets comprising the basket in exchange for a creation unit of shares. This in-kind redemption process generally results in a more tax efficient product than if the ETF sold and redeemed shares in cash, like comparable traditional open-end funds, due to a provision in the Internal Revenue Code that allows funds not to recognize capital gains on securities disposed of in such in-kind transactions.

D. Premium/Discount

Similar to closed-end funds, the secondary market prices of ETF shares may be higher or lower than the ETF's NAV per share. However, the structure of ETFs facilitates arbitrage transactions in ETF shares, and such arbitrage is generally expected to cause the secondary market price of ETF shares to be very close to NAV so that ETFs trade at minimal premiums and discounts to NAV. The ETF arbitrage process is facilitated by ETFs providing portfolio transparency, disclosing the intraday indicative value of the portfolios, and selling and redeeming shares in creation units on a daily basis at NAV. The arbitrage process generally works as follows: an AP, on behalf of itself or a third party, sells short either the ETF's shares or the basket instruments. For example, if the ETF is trading at a discount to NAV, an AP may sell short the instruments in the ETF's basket while buying individual ETF shares in the secondary market. Then, at the end of the day, the AP delivers the creation unit(s) of ETF shares for redemption by the ETF and receives the basket instruments in exchange, which it uses to cover its short sales. This transaction, by decreasing the supply of ETF shares in the secondary market, should help bring the (discounted) secondary market price of the ETF's shares in line with the value of the ETF's portfolio (i.e., NAV).

E. Director Oversight

ETF directors, like all fund directors, have a fiduciary duty to the fund and serve to protect the interests of fund shareholders. As with any open-end fund, directors are responsible for the oversight of an ETF's management and operations. Also as with traditional open-end funds, the directors' responsibilities and oversight practices may vary based on a number of factors, including the nature of the ETF's investments, the ETF's use of leverage and derivatives, and whether the ETF is an index ETF or an active ETF. For example, the method by which the board oversees performance may differ for index ETFs and active ETFs. The boards of index ETFs generally assess performance by the degree to which the ETF was able to track its index, whereas the performance of active ETFs generally is measured against peer group and/or benchmark performance or other performance metrics akin to traditional open-end funds. Unlike open-end funds, however, ETF directors monitor the ETF's market trading, such as premiums and discounts to NAV, intra-day trading spreads and trading volumes. Despite these nuances, similar to traditional fund directors, ETF directors oversee performance and compliance, and they review and approve advisory and distribution contracts, and the continuance thereof, among other responsibilities.

In addition, ETF directors monitor the ETF's compliance with the exemptive relief that permits it to operate as an ETF, as well as any other exemptive orders on which the ETF relies. Certain types of exemptive relief may be the same as that obtained by traditional funds, and the directors' responsibilities would be the same in both situations. For example, like traditional funds, an ETF may lend its securities and use an affiliated lending agent pursuant to an SEC exemptive order. Many ETFs also have exemptive relief that permits other registered funds to invest in the ETFs in excess of the normal limitations imposed by the 1940 Act on investments by registered funds in other registered funds. Some traditional open-end funds also have such exemptive relief. Such relief requires directors in both circumstances to make certain findings and to implement policies and procedures to protect against conflicts of interest.

Other Types of Funds

A. Hedge Funds and Private Investment Companies

In recent years there has been substantial growth in pooled investment entities that are exempt from the registration and reporting requirements of the 1940 Act. These exempt entities are largely private investment companies or so-called hedge funds. In 2012, the Dodd-Frank Act eliminated the private fund adviser exemption to the Investment Advisers Act. These private fund advisers, including advisers to hedge funds, are subject to the same registration, regulatory oversight, and other requirements, such as being subject to examination, that apply to other SEC regulated investment advisers. Since that time, the industry has seen even more of a convergence of registered fund and unregistered fund products, with many registered funds adopting hedge fund-like strategies and advisers to hedge funds entering the registered fund arena.

Many mutual fund sponsors also sponsor private investment companies. The SEC inspection staff has stated that, because the adviser typically receives a percentage of capital gains for managing private investment companies, it may have an incentive to favor private investment companies over registered funds that have a lower advisory fee. The staff has stated that it will examine trade allocations as part of its inspection program to determine if the allocations are conducted in a fair manner. The staff has also stated that it is concerned about the possibility of manipulation resulting from the use of short sales by hedge funds when public funds have long positions in the same security. Fund directors should be satisfied that fund advisers and sub-advisers have compliance procedures in place to address these conflicts of interest and potential for abuse when they advise hedge funds as well as mutual funds.

B. Funds Investing in Foreign Securities

Investment in foreign securities presents several areas for special oversight by fund directors, particularly custody of assets, portfolio valuation and liquidity. To the extent the foreign securities markets in which the fund trades are not as developed or are less efficient than U.S. markets, or to the extent the volume of trading is lower than in the U.S. markets, questions are more likely to arise as to the appropriateness of the valuation of one or more portfolio securities. These issues are not generally relevant for securities traded in developed foreign markets, but can be an issue in certain emerging and frontier markets. These factors also may raise questions as to compliance with portfolio liquidity requirements for open-end funds. Another difficulty in administering funds investing in foreign markets is obtaining timely information as to matters affecting portfolio securities, such as the declaration of dividends and distributions. Directors have specific responsibilities as to the selection of foreign custodians of fund assets (see Section 7.C(1)). In recent years some international funds have experienced issues reclaiming withholding taxes that the funds believe they are entitled to under applicable laws, as some foreign taxation authorities have resisted paying claims made by funds even in the face of favorable court rulings. Certain jurisdictions do not impose withholding taxes but there may be issues about whether funds should accrue liabilities for taxes the liability for which is uncertain. Directors should be kept apprised about such issues, and may be asked to approve expenditures by funds in an effort to pursue claims, which may be for substantial amounts in some cases.

C. Funds Used as Funding Vehicles for Insurance Products

Variable annuity contracts and variable life insurance policies invest in mutual funds that, because of federal income tax limitations, do not offer their shares to the general public but are dedicated to insurance products or tax-qualified retirement plans and are required to satisfy special federal tax diversification requirements. The legal owners of these dedicated fund shares are the insurance company separate accounts, which in many cases are, together with the interests in the insurance products they issue to contract owners, themselves separately regulated under the federal securities laws. The 1940 Act places responsibility on the insurance company, and not the dedicated fund or its board of directors, to determine the reasonableness of aggregate insurance product fees and charges.

There are areas in which dedicated fund boards have duties directly to contract holders as beneficial owners of the fund shares. SEC rules and administrative positions require that voting rights attributable to dedicated fund shares held by the separate account be "passed-through" to contract holders and that fund shares held by the insurance company or otherwise not voted be "echo voted" in proportion to the contract holder votes received. In addition, certain SEC rules provide exemptions to insurance companies offering variable life insurance policies provided that the funds underlying such policies do not sell their shares to both variable annuity separate accounts and variable life separate accounts (known as mixed funding) or sell fund shares to unaffiliated insurance companies (known as shared funding). Many funds have obtained relief from the SEC to permit them to engage in mixed and shared funding while maintaining an insurance company's ability to rely on the exemptions provided under the SEC's rules relating to variable life insurance (known as a mixed and shared funding order). Funds that rely on a mixed and shared funding order must have a majority of independent directors, and the directors must establish and follow procedures to monitor for "irreconcilable material conflicts" that might arise among the interests of contract owners and determine any appropriate action to be taken in the event of a conflict. The SEC recently announced that funds are not required to obtain a mixed and shared funding order prior to offering their shares as an investment option under a variable annuity contract or a variable life insurance policy, and that funds that have previously obtained such an order need not comply with the terms and conditions of that order, if the exemptions granted by the order are not being relied upon by any person.

The laws governing the approval of a mutual fund's investment advisory agreement do not specifically refer to dedicated funds or variable insurance products. However, where a dedicated fund is advised by an insurance company (or an affiliate of an insurance company) issuing insurance products investing in the fund, the relationship between the fund and the insurance company should be considered by the board of directors of the dedicated fund in this context. Also, the SEC staff has taken the position that a board of directors presented with approval of a Rule 12b-1 plan for a dedicated fund must look to the best interests of the ultimate contract owners, not the insurance company separate account nominal shareholders, and assure itself that the 12b-1 plan proceeds are being used for legitimate services supporting the indirect marketing of the dedicated fund shares through the insurance company separate account to contract owners.

The SEC requires insurance company issuers of variable insurance products to deliver to contract owners materials prepared by dedicated funds for their shareholders, including prospectuses, annual and semi-annual reports, proxy materials and other shareholder materials. In addition, one court has held that owners of variable insurance products are "security holders" for purposes of Section 36(b) of the 1940 Act, and therefore have standing to sue investment advisers to dedicated funds for alleged excessive compensation received from the funds.

D. Registered Funds of Hedge Funds

Registered funds of hedge funds are closed-end investment companies, typically organized as either limited partnerships or limited liability companies. These funds principally invest in privately placed, unregistered hedge funds, managed by third-party investment managers. Their goal is to create a diversified portfolio of hedge funds without directly subjecting investors to the underlying funds' minimum investment requirements and the risks associated with a single hedge fund adviser. The SEC staff requires registered funds of hedge funds to be sold only to "accredited investors." In addition, registered funds of hedge funds that charge a performance fee may also be subject to greater restrictions on who can invest and higher investment minimums.

In contrast to typical, publicly traded closed-end funds, investor liquidity is provided by periodic tender offers (often quarterly or semi-annually) at net asset value, rather than by marketplace sales. Secondary sales may be severely limited due either to partnership tax concerns or investor qualification requirements. Because these funds are not publicly traded, and thus are not sold in the secondary markets at a discount to NAV, and because they are not subject to exchange rules requiring annual meetings of stockholders, they do not attract opportunistic investors seeking to profit by pressuring fund boards to take actions to close the discount (see Sections 13.A(4) and 13.H).

Additional benefits of the registered fund of hedge funds structure include: (i) the elimination of the limit on the number of beneficial owners applicable to private funds necessary to establish exemptions from the registration requirements of the 1940 Act; (ii) the exclusion from the FINRA rule that limits participation in "hot" initial public offerings in some instances; (iii) the receipt of favorable pass-through tax treatment as a partnership or, in certain cases, as a RIC; and (iv) the ability of employee benefit plans to invest without creating attendant ERISA concerns.

Directors' responsibilities generally are the same as those of directors of a traditional registered closed-end fund. However, areas for particular focus include avoidance of affiliated transactions, maintaining partnership or, in certain cases RIC, tax status and asset valuation. A fund must avoid engaging in affiliated transactions based on fund ownership of underlying funds or due to the adviser's management of other private funds. A fund seeking partnership tax treatment must not run afoul of the publicly traded partnership rules, which serve to limit transferability of interests and opportunities for their repurchase. A fund seeking RIC status must gain information from underlying funds or limit investment to offshore "PFIC" funds. In addition, registered funds of hedge funds face unique valuation issues. As with other registered investment companies in respect of their non-publicly traded positions, a registered fund of hedge funds must fair value the fund's portfolio holdings (namely, the underlying hedge funds). The process is complicated, because valuations customarily are obtained, without supporting information, from the hedge fund, the manager or general partner of which views the hedge fund's underlying securities positions as proprietary and, thus, ordinarily will not disclose them specifically. For this reason, directors often receive information regarding the fund of hedge fund adviser's process for selecting and monitoring the underlying hedge funds and the adviser's review of the underlying hedge fund manager's valuation procedures.

E. Bank-related Funds

Banks may engage in investment company activities both with respect to their "proprietary funds," which they manage, and "nonproprietary funds," which are managed by others and sold through bank retail channels and bank trust departments.

Affiliates of bank holding companies whose election to be "financial holding companies" is effective may engage in most kinds of fund activities. For the most part, the SEC is the "functional regulator" of bank mutual fund activities.

Directors of bank-related funds should monitor the relationship between banks and their affiliates, on one hand, and the funds that they advise or distribute, on the other. Banking regulations or restrictions still apply to relationships between the banks and their affiliated funds and may present some compliance issues. Directors should inquire about potential conflicts and how management monitors them.

Sales practices are a particular concern for fund shares sold on bank premises. A number of the regulatory authorities and industry associations have issued sales practice guidelines designed to ensure the separation of fund sales activities from insured deposit-taking activities in order to avoid confusion between insured and noninsured products and to foster appropriate qualification, training, and compliance programs.

F. Business Development Companies

Business development companies are a specialized type of closed-end investment company created by Congress in 1980 whose principal activities consist of investing in, and providing "significant managerial assistance" to, small, growing or financially troubled domestic businesses. These companies, which make a special election pursuant to Section 54 of the 1940 Act, enjoy greater operational flexibility in areas including compensation and borrowing as compared to mutual funds or other closed-end funds. However, these companies have strict investment limitations and are subject to reporting requirements like those of public operating companies. Most business development companies sell a fixed number of shares in periodic offerings and provide investors with liquidity by listing their shares on a stock exchange. As business development companies are subject to many, but not all, of the provisions of the 1940 Act, directors are advised to consult appropriate counsel. Special issues relating to business development companies are beyond the scope of this Guidebook.

Liability Limitation, Indemnification, and Insurance

Directors may incur expenses and be at risk for potential personal liability in claims alleging breach of their duties to the fund under state law, as well as in claims alleging failure to satisfy their obligations under the federal securities laws or other applicable laws. A director who is sued for breach of duty or for another violation of law may be exculpated from liability under state law by a provision in the fund's charter, may be entitled to indemnification and advancement of expenses from the fund pursuant to its charter, by-laws, board resolution or an indemnification contract between the fund and its directors, and may be entitled to insurance coverage under a directors' and officers' (D&O) liability insurance policy.

Both the SEC and the ICI best practices report have recommended that a fund board obtain indemnification from the fund and/or D&O liability insurance coverage that is adequate to ensure the independence and effectiveness of the fund's independent directors. Appropriate indemnification and insurance is generally essential to attracting and retaining qualified directors.

A. Limitation of Liability

A significant majority of the state corporation laws (including those of Maryland and Delaware), the Model Act and business trust law permit a fund to include in its charter a provision limiting directors' personal liability to the fund and its shareholders for money damages in suits by the fund or by a shareholder either directly or derivatively. Typically, the availability of this protection is subject to various exceptions set forth in the statute, such as self-dealing or dishonesty. Further, liability limitation does not extend to liability to third parties, claims for nonmonetary or equitable relief or, in particular, violations of the federal securities laws, or other federal laws or the laws of other jurisdictions.

In addition to state law limitations on liability limitation, the 1940 Act restricts a fund's ability to protect or attempt to protect a director from liability to the fund or its shareholders for certain disabling conduct (willful misfeasance, bad faith, gross negligence or reckless disregard of duties). Thus, a fund may not take advantage of state laws that permit the exculpation of liability for misconduct that goes beyond simple negligence.

B. Indemnification

Most state corporation statutes (including Maryland and Delaware) specify the circumstances in which the corporation is permitted or required to indemnify its directors against liability and related reasonable expenses incurred in connection with their service as directors of the corporation. Funds often agree to indemnify directors to the fullest extent permitted by law against liability and reasonable expenses incurred as a result of their service as directors. The permissible indemnification for fund directors depends upon a fund's jurisdiction and form of organization. Fund directors and their counsel should review the specific indemnification provisions applicable to the fund with particular regard to whether indemnification is mandatory or permissible, and the types of proceedings (e.g., civil, criminal or administrative), conduct and time frame covered (e.g., whether protection with respect to prior conduct continues after a director retires).

State law places certain limits on indemnification. Under the Model Act, a director may be indemnified by a corporation only if he has acted in good faith and with a reasonable belief that his conduct was in the best interests of the corporation. In the case of criminal proceedings, the director must also have had no reasonable cause to believe his conduct was unlawful. The Model Act also permits a corporation to provide in its charter or bylaws or by contract for broader indemnification, subject to certain limitations. However, as noted above, the 1940 Act prohibits a fund from indemnifying its directors for liability to the fund or its shareholders arising from the directors' willful misfeasance, bad faith, gross negligence or reckless disregard of duties. The SEC staff interprets this provision to require a fund to use "reasonable and fair means" to determine whether the disabling conduct exists. According to the staff, "reasonable and fair means" would include: (i) a final decision by a court or other body on the merits, (ii) a reasonable determination based upon a review of the facts by a vote of a majority of the disinterested directors not involved in the proceeding, or (iii) such a reasonable determination by an independent legal counsel in a written opinion. The SEC also takes the position that indemnification for liabilities arising under the 1933 Act "is against public policy."

C. Advancement of Expenses

Most state corporation statutes specify the circumstances in which a corporation may advance funds to a director to pay or reimburse reasonable expenses incurred by the director in defense of a matter prior to the final disposition of the proceeding and before final determination of the director's right to indemnification for those expenses. A director generally must provide the corporation with a written undertaking that any funds advanced by the corporation will be repaid if it is ultimately determined that the director is not entitled to indemnification.

In addition, the SEC staff takes the position that prior to an advance: (i) the director must give security for the advance; (ii) the fund must have insurance against losses arising from lawful advances; or (iii) the disinterested nonparty directors, or independent legal counsel in a written opinion, must determine that the director would be entitled to indemnification. In making a determination that an independent director would be entitled to indemnification (and, therefore, entitled to advancement of expenses), the SEC staff has taken the position that the disinterested nonparty directors, or independent legal counsel, may rebuttably presume that such an independent director did not engage in disabling conduct. In addition, state law often requires the director to sign a good faith affirmation that the director meets the applicable standard for indemnification.

D. Insurance Issues

Although not required by law, many funds purchase and maintain Directors and Officers ("D&O") liability insurance, which typically (1) protects fund directors and officers directly for losses they incur in covered claims where fund indemnification is otherwise unavailable to them (sometimes referred to as "direct" or "Side A" coverage), and (2) covers the fund itself for amounts payable by the fund as indemnification to directors and officers in covered claims where fund indemnification is available to them (sometimes referred to as "company reimbursement" or "Side B" coverage). D&O liability insurance is also often coupled with errors and omissions (E&O) liability insurance, which protects the fund for claims made against the fund itself.

Not all D&O/E&O policies are the same. Coverage, terms and conditions may vary significantly, depending upon the policy and the insurer. The key areas of difference among D&O/E&O policies may include: (i) the types of claims covered (e.g., whether "informal" government investigations are covered); (ii) the types of wrongful acts covered and/ or excluded; (iii) the circumstances under which defense costs will be advanced by the insurer; and (iv) when notice of a claim must be given.

A D&O/E&O policy allows the fund to protect itself against its potential liability to its directors (and officers) for indemnification and advance of expenses, as well as offering further protection to directors (and officers) against potential defense costs and liabilities that may result from their service to the fund. The availability of insurance may be important if, for instance, the fund is insolvent or is unable to indemnify former directors, or if state or federal law limits indemnification or advancement of expenses or if the board refuses to authorize payment.

In structuring a D&O/E&O insurance program, directors may wish to consider a number of factors, including: (i) whether to obtain a "funds only" policy or a "joint" policy with the funds' adviser and/or other parties; (ii) the size of the policy, the deductible and the premiums charged; (iii) the reputation and claims paying history of the insurer; (iv) whether to obtain a "single-insurer" or "multiple-insurer" (layered) program; and (v) the scope of the insuring clauses and the exclusions.

Funds often purchase "joint" D&O/E&O polices with other funds in their complex and/or with the funds' adviser, underwriter and/or other affiliates. Joint coverage is permitted under the 1940 Act if certain requirements are met, including that the board of directors of each covered fund make certain determinations, and that the independent directors and their counsel meet the minimum independence requirements set forth in the SEC Governance Standards discussed in Sections 4.A(2) and 4.C(6). The primary advantage of a joint policy is that it usually enables all parties to obtain a greater amount of overall coverage at a relatively lower premium. In determining the appropriate amount of total coverage under a joint policy, however, directors should consider the risk that the limits of the policy may be exhausted by claims made against other insureds. Directors can seek to protect themselves from this "exhaustion" risk in various ways, including reserving a portion of the joint policy exclusively for the directors of their fund or obtaining a stand-alone independent director policy (IDL), which is exclusively for independent directors.

In addition, a joint policy requires the directors to approve the allocation of the premium among the parties. Under the applicable rule, the portion of the premium to be allocated to a fund, based on its proportionate share of the sum of the premiums that would have been paid if the insured parties purchased such insurance coverage separately, must be fair and reasonable to the fund. Fund boards may seek an estimate from the insurer of the costs of separate policies for the funds versus a joint policy along with a suggested premium split. The premium split may vary among fund complexes, and often the parties will apply a higher percentage to the adviser/underwriter than to the funds (e.g., 60%/40%). Directors must exercise their business judgment in considering a recommended split, and take into account the fact that if the adviser or its affiliates are a party that they have a conflict of interest in recommending a split. Directors also sometimes approve an "allocation agreement" among the insured parties, which addresses the allocations and priority of recoveries under the joint policy.

Fund directors may also wish to consider whether to obtain "tail coverage" or other indemnification or insurance for funds that may be liquidated or merged (see Section 7.D(2) for further discussion of fund liquidations and mergers).

Appendix A

Regulatory Calendar

This outline sets forth significant matters for which fund boards of directors or their audit committee(s) have responsibilities under the 1940 Act, the Sarbanes-Oxley Act, or the Dodd-Frank Act along with references to such matters in this Guidebook. In addition, the directors may have duties that are specified in the terms and conditions of an exemptive order or an interpretative or no-action letter.

1) Management Arrangements
   —Approve management/investment advisory agreements—Section 5
   —Approve sub-advisory agreements—Section 5.D
   —Approve service contracts with affiliates—Section 5.E
   —Review of disclosure as to board evaluation of advisory arrangements—Section 5.C
2) Distribution Arrangements
   —Approve distribution agreements—Section 6
   —Approve Rule 12b-1 distribution plans—Section 6
   —Approve multi-class arrangements (Rule 18f-3)—Section 6.D(4)
   —Review of revenue sharing arrangements and payments to intermediaries—Section 6.C and 6.D(8)
   —Approve policies and procedures to permit use of a broker-dealer who sells shares of the fund—Section 6.D(5)
   —Determination of whether to impose a redemption fee—Section 6.D(6)

3) Financial Reporting Matters
   —Selection and oversight of independent accountants—Section 4.B(1)(b), 7.C(3)
   —Audit committee charter—Section 7.C(3), Section 13.G(1)
   —Review accountant's annual written report to the audit committee—Section 4.B(1)(b)
   —Approval of non-audit services—Section 4.B(1)(b)
   —Identify "audit committee financial experts"—Section 4.B(1)(a)
4) Compliance Program
   —Approve and oversee compliance policies and procedures—Section 9.A and C
   —Approve appointment and compensation of the chief compliance officer (CCO)—Section 9.B
   —Review annual written report of CCO—Section 9.B
5) Governance Matters
   —Determination of independence of counsel for the independent directors—Section 4.C(6)
   —Explicitly authorize the independent directors to hire employees and to retain advisers and experts necessary to carry out their duties—Section 4.C(6)
   —Conduct annual self-assessment of board performance—Section 4.C(7)
   —Selection and nomination of independent directors—Section 4.B(2)
6) Disclosure Matters
   —Review and sign the registration statements of the fund filed with the SEC in connection with the fund's offering of securities to the public—Section 11.A
   —Provide fund management with information (whether through a questionnaire or otherwise) to enable fund management to accurately prepare registration statements, proxy statements and other disclosures concerning the director and to determine on a continuous basis the director's status as an "interested person"—Section 4.A(4)
7) Operational Responsibilities
   —Monitor investment practices including the use of derivatives and alternative strategies—Section 7.B(1) and Section 10
   —Monitor portfolio trading practices—Section 7.B(2)
   —Monitor the use of soft dollars—Section 7.B(3)

—Approve policies and procedures to ensure that the selection of brokers is not influenced by fund share distribution considerations—Section 6.D(5)

—Monitor trade allocation practices—Section 7.B(4)

—Approve methodologies used for valuation of portfolio securities and pricing of fund shares—Section 8.B

—Monitor the use of fair value pricing—Section 8.B

—Monitor guidelines and standards for determining portfolio liquidity—Section 7.B(6)

—Oversee custody arrangements with specific obligations with respect to self-custody, affiliated custody and foreign custody arrangements—Section 7.C(1)

—Approval of the fidelity bond arrangements and the allocation of premiums on joint insurance policies—Section 7.C(2), 16.D

—Approve and monitor procedures required by exemptive rules relating to fund securities transactions involving affiliates—Section 7.B(7)

—Approve and monitor securities lending programs and guidelines—Section 7.B(8)

—Monitor guidelines related to special types of investment practices including repurchase agreements, reverse repurchase agreements and futures contracts—Section 7.B(9)

—Monitor the extent to which the fund utilizes leverage—Section 7.B(10)

—Make determinations with respect to money market fund valuation and credit quality procedures required by Rule 2a-7—Section 12

—Monitor the proxy voting policies and procedures and the proxy voting record of the fund—Section 11.A(4)

—Approve policies and procedures related to market timing and monitor policies and procedures as to selective disclosure of portfolio securities—Section 7.C(13)

—Consideration of measures to address the tendency of closed-end fund shares to trade at a discount—Section 13.H(2)

8) Other Responsibilities

—Compliance with codes of ethics under the 1940 Act and Sarbanes-Oxley Act—Section 7.C(4)

—Approval of the fund's anti-money laundering program—Section 7.C(6)

—Monitor the manner in which the fund and the adviser seek to ensure compliance with representation and conditions continued in SEC exemptive orders or no-action or interpretative letters—Section 7.A(1)
—Monitor the manner in which the fund and the adviser and its affiliates are complying with the fund's whistleblower program (including the anti-retaliation provisions) Section 7.C(12)

Glossary

Administrator: Entity that provides administrative but not investment advisory services to a fund.

Advisers Act: The Investment Advisers Act of 1940, as amended, which regulates investment advisers to funds.

Affiliated Persons: Categories of persons specified in Section 2(a)(3) of the 1940 Act as having specific degrees of affiliation with another person, such as owning 5% or more of the voting securities of such person (or vice versa), having control or common control relationships, or acting as an officer, director, or employee of the other person.

Amortized Cost Method of Valuation: A method of valuation available to certain money market funds to facilitate the maintenance of a constant net asset value permitted by Rule 2a-7 pursuant to which portfolio securities are valued at the fund's acquisition cost adjusted for amortization of premium or accretion of discount rather than at current market value.

Anti-Money Laundering Program: Program, procedures, and internal controls reasonably designed to prevent a fund from being used for money laundering or the financing of terrorist activities under the USA PATRIOT Act.

Audit Committee: A committee of the board of directors consisting of independent directors that has responsibilities with respect to the retention and oversight of the fund's auditors and the review of the fund's financial statements and other financial reporting matters.

Audit Committee Financial Expert: A term defined by the SEC to denote members of the audit committee that have been determined by the fund's board to have specified attributes as a result of having specified experience.

Bank-Related Fund: A fund that is managed by a bank or sold through bank distribution channels.

BDCs: Business development companies, which are a specialized type of closed-end investment company whose principal activities consist of investing in, and providing "significant managerial assistance" to, small, growing, or financially troubled domestic businesses.

Chief Compliance Officer: The chief compliance officer, or CCO, is responsible for administering the compliance program for the fund under Rule 38a-1 under the 1940 Act and for the investment adviser under Rule 206(4)-7 under the Advisers Act.

Closed-end Fund: A fund whose shares are non-redeemable. The shares of most closed-end funds trade in the secondary market at prices which are not tied to net asset value.

Codes of Ethics: The rules under the 1940 Act require funds, investment advisers and distributors to adopt a code of ethics designed to prevent persons with access to information as to fund portfolio security activities from engaging in fraudulent, deceptive or manipulative trading practices. The Sarbanes-Oxley Act requires disclosure as to whether a fund has adopted a code of ethics that covers a broader range of ethical conduct by its CEO and principal financial officer. The two codes can be integrated.

Commodity Pool: An investment trust, syndicate, or similar form of enterprise operated for purposes of trading in commodity interests, including commodity futures contracts and options thereon, retail off-exchange foreign exchange contracts, or swaps (excluding certain security-based swaps), or to invest in another commodity pool. The operator and each advisor of a commodity pool must be registered with, and are subject to regulation by, the CFTC and NFA as a CPO or CTA, respectively, unless otherwise exempted or excluded pursuant to the CEA or CFTC regulations. A fund is generally a commodity pool if it has the ability to utilize commodity interests unless an exclusion pursuant to CFTC Rule 4.5 is available.

Commodity Pool Operator (CPO):   An individual or organization engaged in a business similar to a commodity pool and who solicits, accepts, or receives funds, securities, or other property from participants for purposes of trading in commodity interests. The operator may either make its own trading decisions on behalf of the pool or engage a CTA to do so. The CFTC takes the position that the fund's adviser is the CPO of a fund that is a commodity pool.

Commodity Trading Advisor (CTA):   An individual or organization which, for compensation or profit, engages in the business of advising others, either directly or indirectly, as to the value of or advisability of trading in commodity interests, or engages in the regular business of issuing or promulgating analyses or reports concerning the value of or advisability of trading in commodity interests. The CTA of a fund is often its adviser, which is also, according to CFTC guidance, the fund's CPO.

Custody Arrangements: Custody arrangements generally refer to the manner in which the assets of a fund are held. The 1940 Act requires that the securities of a fund be maintained in the custody of a qualified custodian. There are special provisions related to custody of assets held outside the United States, in domestic or foreign securities depositories, by futures commission merchants and commodity clearing organizations, and in other special situations.

Dark Pools: Refers to alternative trading systems that do not publicly display quotations in the consolidated market quotation data.

Distributor: The entity responsible for selling the shares of the mutual fund, which may, in turn, contract with brokers/dealers and other intermediaries for the sale of fund shares to the public. The distributor is referred to in the 1940 Act as the "principal underwriter". The distribution arrangements of a mutual fund are subject to regulation under the 1940 Act and the sales practices generally are subject to regulation by FINRA.

Diversified: A diversified fund is limited by the 1940 Act as to the proportion of its assets that it may invest in securities of a single issuer. Funds must elect, under the 1940 Act, to be classified as a diversified or non-diversified fund.

Dodd-Frank Act: The Dodd-Frank Wall Street Reform and Consumer Protection Act, which mandates a series of federal regulations affecting financial institutions and their customers primarily intended to attempt to prevent the recurrence of events that caused the 2008 financial crisis and lower risk in various parts of the U.S. financial system.

Exchange Traded Fund (ETF): A term not defined in the 1940 Act, which is commonly used to refer to a hybrid investment company, legally classified as an open-end company or UIT, whose shares are traded intra-day on a securities exchange at a market-determined price that may or may not be the same as their NAV, similar to shares of a listed closed-end fund. ETFs of this type are regulated by the SEC and subject to oversight by boards of directors. Other ETFs that invest primarily in commodity interests, such as physical metals, are not funds and are not required to register under the 1940 Act, although they register their shares and file reports with the SEC. These types of ETFs are beyond the scope of this Guidebook.

Expense Ratio: Ratio, usually expressed as a percentage, that compares annual fund expenses for management fees and other operating expenses to the average net asset value of a fund's outstanding shares during the year.

Fair Value Pricing: Method of valuation for pricing purposes to be used when market prices of portfolio securities are not available or may not be reliable, including due to events occurring subsequent to the close of trading but prior to a fund's determination of NAV.

Fidelity Bond: The bond which each fund must maintain against larceny or embezzlement. The form and amount of the bond are subject to 1940 Act regulation.

FINRA: Financial Industry Regulatory Authority is a self-regulatory organization of almost all securities firms, which is subject to SEC jurisdiction and oversight. FINRA regulates, among other things, the sales practices of broker/dealers selling shares of funds.

Fund: See "Investment Company."

Fund of Funds: An investment company organized to invest in other investment companies.

Hedge Funds: See "Private Investment Companies."

High Frequency Trading: A program trading platform that uses powerful computers to transact a large number of orders at very fast speed.

Independent Director: A fund director who is not an "interested person" of the investment company as defined in Section 2(a)(19) of the 1940 Act. Members of the audit committee are subject to further independence requirements under the Sarbanes-Oxley Act.

Interested Persons: Any one of several categories of persons specified in Section 2(a)(19) of the 1940 Act having interests potentially in conflict with the fund. The "interested person" category is broader than the "affiliated person" category.

Intermediaries: Broker-dealers, banks, retirement plan administrators, and other institutions that operate platforms through which investors in mutual funds buy and sell their shares.

Interval Fund: A closed-end fund that is permitted, pursuant to a rule under the 1940 Act, to make periodic mandatory repurchase offers without having to comply with the SEC's tender offer rules.

Investment Adviser: The entity responsible for the portfolio management, and typically other matters necessary for the operation of the fund, including oversight of service providers. The investment adviser may be referred to as the adviser, manager, investment manager or some other variation thereof. Management arrangements may be split between the adviser and an administrator or a sub-adviser (which assumes specified advisor responsibilities). The management arrangements are regulated under the 1940 Act and the activities of investment advisers and sub-advisers are also subject to regulation under the Advisers Act.

Investment Company: An entity investing in securities that sells its shares to the public, is registered under the 1940 Act, and is subject to regulation thereunder. Certain investment companies, such as those offered privately with fewer than 100 security holders or only to investors meeting certain qualifications ("private investment companies" or "hedge funds") and funds organized in jurisdictions outside the United States and principally sold to foreign investors ("offshore funds"), are exempt from 1940 Act registration.

ICI: The Investment Company Institute, which is the national association of the American investment company industry.

ICI Best Practices Report: The Investment Company Institute-sponsored "best practices report," developed by an advisory group and published in 1999, identifying a variety of corporate governance practices beyond those required by law.

IDC: The Independent Directors Council, which was established by the ICI in 2004 and aims to advance the education, communication, and policy positions of fund independent directors and promote public understanding of their role.

Late Trading: The unlawful practice of placing orders to buy or redeem mutual fund shares after 4:00 p.m. Eastern time, as of which most funds calculate their net asset value ("NAV"), but receiving the price based on the 4:00 p.m. NAV.

Listing Requirements: The listing requirements for closed-end funds with securities listed on a stock exchange. Certain requirements of the Sarbanes-Oxley Act are implemented through the listing requirements of the national securities exchanges. Although not applicable to open-end funds, the listing requirements may serve as a "best practices" guide for open-end funds.

Load Fund: A fund that imposes a sales charge in connection with the sale of its shares.

Manager: See "Investment Adviser."

Market Timing: The practice of rapid in-and-out trades in fund shares in order to take advantage of time zone, currency conversion or other forms of pricing discrepancies inherent in the fund NAV calculation. Market timing itself is not an illegal practice but may involve abusive or fraudulent activities, and many funds have policies and procedures, which may include limitations on transactions or the imposition of redemption fees, that are designed to prevent market timing transactions because the activities of market timers are believed to impose unwarranted costs on long term fund shareholders.

Master-feeder Fund: Two-tier fund structure involving an underlying fund ("master fund") and any number of first-tier funds ("feeder funds") having as their sole investment an investment in the underlying SEC-registered master fund. The various feeder funds need not necessarily be 1940 Act entities and each may have different distribution arrangements.

Money Market Fund: Fund that invests in short-term money market instruments and offers investors relative safety of principal, a high degree of liquidity, a wide range of shareholder services (including check-writing), and that have historically sought to maintain a stable net asset value (usually $1.00 per share). Such funds are sometimes referred to as money funds. The shares of the money fund may either be taxable ("taxable money fund") or exempt from federal taxation ("tax-free money fund"), depending primarily upon whether the portfolio money market securities are taxable or tax-exempt. As a result of significant reforms adopted by the SEC in 2014, which are being phased in through 2016, some money funds will no longer be able to maintain a stable NAV.

Multiple-class Fund: A mutual fund that issues separate classes of shares each with a different distribution arrangement but each representing interests in the same portfolio of securities.

Mutual Fund: A term not defined in the 1940 Act that is commonly used to refer to an open-end fund.

MFDF: The Mutual Fund Directors Forum, which is an independent organization devoted to educating and furthering the views of investment company independent directors.

MFDF Best Practices Report: A report published in July 2004 and updated in 2013 containing recommended best practices and practical guidance for mutual fund directors on board review of management arrangements and other fund-related matters.

Net Asset Value Per Share: The price at which purchases and redemptions of shares of open-end funds are transacted. The net asset value per share is computed by dividing the sum of the value of the securities held by the fund plus any cash or other assets (including accrued interest and dividends receivable) minus all liabilities (including accrued expenses) by the total number of shares outstanding at the time of determination. Often referred to as "NAV."

1933 Act: The Securities Act of 1933, as amended, a disclosure statute designed to ensure that investors are provided with full and fair disclosure of material information in connection with the offering and sale of securities, including fund shares.

1934 Act: The Securities Exchange Act of 1934, as amended, which regulates the securities markets and broker-dealers as well as imposing ongoing reporting and proxy requirements on public companies. Some of the provisions of the Sarbanes-Oxley Act are set forth in the 1934 Act.

1940 Act: The Investment Company Act of 1940, as amended, which contains comprehensive provisions regulating investment companies registered thereunder.

No-load Fund: A fund that sells its shares at net asset value without any sales charge.

Non-diversified: See "Diversified."

Omnibus Accounts: Aggregated accounts where an intermediary has one or more accounts with a mutual fund's transfer agent and the intermediary maintains the underlying shareholder account information and manages all interactions with and servicing of the underlying shareholders.

Open-end Fund: A fund that issues shares redeemable at net asset value at any time at the option of the shareholder and typically engages in a continuous offering of its shares. Open-end funds are commonly referred to as "mutual funds."

Penny-rounding Method of Pricing: A method of pricing historically available to money market funds to facilitate the maintenance of a constant net asset value permitted by Rule 2a-7 in which the current net asset value is rounded to the nearest 1%. As a result of reforms adopted by the SEC in 2014, by late 2016 certain types of money market funds will no longer be permitted to maintain a stable NAV.

Pricing: The daily process of determining the price at which open-end fund shares are sold and redeemed which is based upon the net asset value of the shares.

Principal Underwriter: The term used in the 1940 Act to denote the person principally responsible for selling the shares of the fund. The principal underwriter is frequently referred to as the distributor.

Private Investment Companies: Pooled investment entities exempt from the registration and reporting requirements of the 1940 Act. See "Investment Company."

PCAOB: The Public Company Accounting Oversight Board is a private-sector, non-profit corporation created by the Sarbanes-Oxley Act to oversee the audits of public companies and other issuers in order to protect the interests of investors. PCAOB inspections assess compliance with certain laws, rules, and professional standards in connection with firms' audits of issuers. The PCAOB is subject to the oversight of the SEC.

Redemption: The term refers to the requirement that open-end funds must redeem shares each business day at the redemption price per share, which is based upon the net asset value per share next determined after receipt of the notice of redemption from the shareholder. The manner in which redemptions are handled is regulated under the 1940 Act.

Regulated Investment Company: The tax term denoting a fund that qualifies for the special flow-through tax treatment afforded under subchapter M of the Internal Revenue Code. Funds that so qualify are entitled to deduct from their taxable income the part of the income distributed to shareholders.

Revenue Sharing: A broad concept, sometimes referred to as payments for "shelf space," related to many types of payments by the fund's adviser or distributor, out of its own resources, to broker-dealers or other intermediaries, in addition to standard sales loads or Rule 12b-1 fees, for the promotion and sale of fund shares by way of financial incentives.

Rule 12b-1 Plan: A distribution plan adopted pursuant to Rule 12b-1 under the 1940 Act, which specifies conditions pursuant to which an open-end fund may use its own assets for marketing or promotional purposes in the sale of fund shares.

Rule 2a-7:   The rule under the 1940 Act that contains comprehensive provisions regulating funds that hold themselves out as money market funds. Among other things, Rule 2a-7 requires money market funds to satisfy detailed requirements as to portfolio quality, maturity and diversification.

Sales Charges: Charges imposed in connection with the sale of mutual fund shares, which can be imposed at the time of sale (a front-end load) or on a deferred basis pursuant to a Rule 12b-1 plan or contingent deferred sales charges.

Sarbanes-Oxley Act: The Sarbanes-Oxley Act of 2002, which contains sweeping reforms affecting, among other things, the oversight of financial reporting by public companies, including funds.

SEC: The Securities and Exchange Commission, the federal regulatory agency responsible for administering the federal securities laws, including the 1940 Act and the Advisers Act. The powers of the SEC include the interpretation, supervision and enforcement of the 1940 Act and the Advisers Act. The SEC staff regularly conducts detailed inspections of funds and investment advisers.

SEC Governance Standards: A special set of governance standards which apply to funds that have adopted Rule 12b-1 plans, issue multiple classes of shares, or rely on any of eight other widely used SEC exemptive rules to engage in certain types of transactions with affiliates. The exemptive rules include a number of rules, which ease the prohibitions on portfolio and other transactions involving affiliates.

Selective Disclosure: The generally illegal practice of disclosing material, non-public information to analysts and institutional investors before releasing it to the public.

Series Fund: A fund that issues shares in multiple series, each of which is in effect a separate fund typically with separate investment objectives and policies.

Shelf Space: See "Revenue Sharing."

Soft Dollars: The use of brokerage commissions to pay for research products and services in addition to trade execution, clearance and settlement. Section 28(e) of the 1934 Act creates a safe harbor that permits advisers to use client commissions to pay for brokerage and research services, subject to various conditions.

Sponsor: The entity which causes the organization and promotion of the investment company.

Subchapter M: This subsection of the Internal Revenue Code containing the provisions that establish the requirements for qualifications for taxation as a regulated investment company. See "Regulated Investment Company."

Unit Investment Trust: A trust registered as an investment company under the 1940 Act, which generally has a fixed portfolio of securities and issues redeemable securities. A UIT does not have a board of directors.

The USA PATRIOT Act: The USA PATRIOT Act of 2001, which requires funds to adopt anti-money laundering and customer identification programs.

Whistleblower: An employee or "agent" who has provided information about possible fraud or violations of federal law to enforcement authorities and others, against whom it is unlawful for a fund to retaliate against (so-called whistleblower protection).

Keyword Index